# Witchcraft

## Theory and Practice

## No Turning Back

*Once you have chosen to take upon yourself the
obligations of the practice of Witchcraft, then the effects,
or the immanence, of this way of life will be bestowed
on you from aligned intelligences, and so will the
tests that accompany them.*

*Anyone who willingly opens themselves to powers
beyond the veil of manifestation (as we understand it)
opens themselves to the possibility of inner initiation.
Witches* know *that they are witches, but initiation is
what seals that knowledge through the power of ritual
and the intent inherent within the process itself, to a deeper
strata of recognition and response both within oneself and
from the powers to which we are oathed.*

*Once initiation has occurred, there is no turning back—you
will quest all your life; it is not a thing to do thoughtlessly.*

—Ly de Angeles

RITUALS, SPELLCASTING & SORCERY

*Theory and Practice*

LY DE ANGELES

2004
Llewellyn Publications
St. Paul, Minnesota 55164-0383, U.S.A.

FIRST EDITION
Ninth Printing, 2004

Cover design by Lisa Novak
Editing by Deb Gruebele
Formatting by Deb Gruebele

Library of Congress Cataloging-in-Publication Data
De Angeles, Ly.
    Witchcraft: theory and practice / by Ly de Angeles
        p. cm.
    Includes bibliographical references.
    ISBN 1–55718–782–X
     1. Witchcraft. I. Title
    BF1566.W37 2000
    133.4'3—dc21

                                            00–041953
                                                  CIP

Llewellyn Worldwide does not participate in, endorse, or have any authority or responsibility concerning private business transactions between our authors and the public.
    All mail addressed to the author is forwarded but the publisher cannot, unless specifically instructed by the author, give out an address or phone number.

Llewellyn Publications
A Division of Llewellyn Worldwide, Ltd.
P. O. Box 64383, Dept. 1–56718–782–x
St. Paul, MN  55164-0383, USA
www.llewellyn.com

 Printed on recycled paper in the United States of America

" . . . and when you *know* the magic believes in you,
how can you not?"

—Ly de Angeles

# CONTENTS

xv    *Prologue*
xix   *Introduction to the Revised Edition*
xxi   *Introduction*


## PART ONE: THE DISCIPLINES

3     **Section One: First Stage Technique Requirements**

3     The Center

6     Meditation

7     Meditation and Ritual

7     Thought, Telepathy, and the Matrix—
      The Key to Manifestation

10    Contemplation

10    Silence

11    Visualization

17    **Section Two: Never to Walk in Anyone's Shadow**

17    Self-Analysis Techniques

29    Mulengro

30    Notes on Human Nature

32    Fear

35    The Ethics of Personal Power

37    Awareness

37    Preparation

38    Intent

38    Focus

39    Personal Power

40    Service

41    The Law of Congruity

42    On Passion


PART TWO: THE WAY OF THE GODDESS

47    **Section One: Required Understanding
      Preparatory to the Practice of Ritual**

47    To Be Witch

50    Do As Ye Will, E'er it Harm None

53    Goddess and God of My Priesthood

56    A Witch's Goddess

57    Full Moon

57    New Moon

58    Dark Moon

58    The Four Fire Festivals
      (Known as the Greater Sabbats)

59    Essential Symbolism of the Four Fire Festivals

60    A Witch's God

61    Solstice and Equinox
      (Known as the Four Lesser Sabbats)

62    Essential Symbolism of Solstice and Equinox

63    The Eight-Fold Wheel of the Year

68    The Elements (Part 2)—Significance in Ritual and
      in the Way of the Sacred

73    A Witch's Most-Valued Possessions
      (The Instruments, Tools, and Weapons of the Art)

78    Keeping Records—
      The Book of Shadows and Various Grimoires

81    The Hermetic Quaternary

**85    Section Two: Ritual Proper**

85    Reiving

87    Ritual—Phase One: To Cast a Ritual Circle

93    Phase Two: Consecration and
      Empowering Your Athame

94    The Rite

98    Phase Three: The Process of Self-Initiation

99    The Ritual

**113   Section Three: Second Stage
      Technique Progressive**

113   Realms of Accessibility

122   Relevant Notes on Qabbalah

124   The Tree

124   The Glyph

127   The Divisions of the Soul (The Body of the Tree)

129   The Four Worlds

130   The Essential Four Worlds

131   The Principle of Creation

132   Time and the Four Worlds


PART THREE: SPELLCRAFTING (SORCERY)

**137   Section One: Application**

137   Letting Go

| | |
|---|---|
| 138 | Fith-fathing |
| 141 | The Rite |
| 146 | Familiars |
| 146 | Fetches |
| 148 | The Rite |
| 152 | Shapeshifting (Therianthropism) |
| 155 | Glamouring |
| 159 | Reivings, Banishings, and Wards (Including Seals and Sigils) |
| 163 | Reiving (Clearing a Place) |
| 164 | Banishing (Getting Rid of a Thing) |
| 165 | Warding (Keeping a Thing Out) |
| 167 | Sigils as Seals |
| 168 | Dreamwalker (Including Astral Projection) |
| 171 | Astral Projection (O.B.E.—Out-of-Body Experience) |
| 172 | Techniques |
| 175 | Omens and Portents (Including More About the Geas) |
| 181 | The Art of Invisibility |
| 182 | The Rite |
| 185 | Psi-Empathy and Psychic Protection |
| 186 | Vampirism |
| 188 | Ghosts and Hauntings |
| 189 | Getting and Hexing (The Hows, Whys, Pros, and Cons) |
| 193 | The Circles of Light and Dark |
| 196 | Training—A Year and a Day Thrice Over |

197    The Three Degrees of Priesthood
202    Author's Note
206    End Notes

**209    Section Two: References**
209    Planetary Symbolism
215    Tarot (Major Arcana)
217    Time
219    Major Arcana
227    The Time Sequences of the Solar/Earth Wheel
       (According to the Major Arcana)
228    Number Symbolism

233    *Table of Correspondences: The Elements*
234    *Table of Correspondences: Planetary Symbols*
237    *Recommended Reading List*
237    *Non-Fiction*
242    *Fiction (Contemporary Folklore)*
245    *Index*

# PROLOGUE

Within the corner of a darkened room a woman sits on a chair and hums a repetitive tune. Her eyes are closed and she rocks back and forth, back and forth, back and forth—seeming to sway in some invisible wind like the rushes on a lake shore. Her hands are moving between threads as she weaves and plaits them, every now and then stopping to tie a knot; the silence more permeable for the lack of song.

She sits, thus, for hours until the room lightens with the glow of the rising Moon, the shafts of which pierce the window to land at her feet. The monotonous humming stops, the rocking stops, the dancing fingers stop—her eyes are open.

She stands and walks to the center of the little room where her table is set with the instruments of her birthright: **cup**, picking up the glow of moonlight and dripping it onto the cloth beneath; **knife** with the hilt as black as jet that glints with streaks of silver that have been set into the ancient runes that surround the base, and with a double-edged blade that flares and tapers finely to its point of power; **pentacle** that glows with burnished light, the symbols on its face deep and meaningless to any save its owner; **wand** of willow wood, finely carved with her own hand into an intricate set of spirals and swirls, worn in places where it has been lovingly worked; unlit **candles** of purest white to compliment the Moon's glow, and a heavy silver **medallion** on a cord, older than even she knows, that has been passed down, along with her knowledge and her **sword**, the Initiator, from one to the other, in secret nights and ancient tongue, from one to another, by right of succession and ancient oath, until to her it was bequeathed with all that belongs to the passage; a **bowl** of burning coals that glow and shed warmth round about, upon which she drops juniper twigs and wood from the dead bough of an apple tree. From the coals she lights a taper, then the candles, one by one—all in silence and certainty of what is to follow.

Her shapeless dress is unbuttoned and dropped to the floor; her hair, bound about her head in a tight braid, is unraveled and spreads around her in a wild, burnished copper haze. The medallion she takes lovingly in her hands to greet with a soft kiss before raising it to the Moon's glow for approval; she then drops its cord over her head onto her breast, drawing comfort from its familiar coldness on her skin.

She kneels, raises her arms above her head, breathes deeply, and waits. Very soon the Moon is fully risen and the shafts of silver cover her body and radiate around her. She cries out, in the ancient tongue of the Lands of Lirian, that she is ready to greet her Goddess, whose name she summons by the name she knows, and it rings around her thrice, like the secret chiming of bells.

The air is still and expectant.

She slowly stands and takes the cup, this sacred chalice, now filled with water, later wine, and walks around the little room sprinkling as she goes. A soft, melodious chant is rising, rising from her as she quickens her pace, deosil, deosil, leaving trails of moonlight glowing in a circle all around her. She feels the force field, an almost imperceptible swishing that grows to a hum. When it is constant she stops, moves back to her table, proclaiming it altar. Now she dips her wand into the cup and uses the sacred water to seal her body from all things impure or mundane, thinking, "Be ye far from us, oh ye profane . . ."[1] She kisses the wand's tip and lays it back on the altar. She refuels the brazier and inhales the sweet-smelling smoke—a tribute to her Goddess. She takes the pentacle between her two hands and raises it above her head, calling forth the force of the Four Winds to act as sentinels to her rite. She takes the dagger, the power of her birthright, and presses it to her breast to fill it with her own essence, and then she stands. The dagger is now athame. She raises it slowly; her whole being is poured from its magnetized tip in shafts of blue fire as it pierces the night for the acknowledgement she knows will come.

Her breath is still. The night is still. The forces of life wait expectantly, and suddenly the light returns to flood the room— the priestess of the Moon cries out to the primordial mother, to whom she was bequeathed before the dawn of time.

The mother answers with the heartbeat of a thousand million lives and acknowledges her daughter, sister, self. They fuse and are one—was it ever any other way?

The cycle is complete, and the priestess of the Moon is assured. The magic of her fingers will soothe where they lay, and the magic of her voice will heal where it is heard, the magic of her eyes will light the Earth, and all things will grow where're she looks upon them.

The Way of the Goddess will continue, though to most her name is unknown. As long as even one remembers will the knowledge proceed and the Earth be sustained.

Though the foolish fear what they don't understand, the magic goes on and the secret survives, for the priestess of the Moon is witch, and what she represents is at one with what's living, and all that she is will continue—for without her the Earth would weep and the night would never understand and so would cease to be. She is the spiral of life—the oceans, the rivers, the falling of the dew, the changing of the seasons. She is the corn at harvest and the birth of birds. She is the wind on the mountain and the spider's web at dawn.

All things of beauty are the name that she summons, for she is the mirror of the Goddess that is life, and the mother of all living things. If she could not continue, or was the last of all, then all hope would cease to be.

# INTRODUCTION TO THE
# REVISED EDITION

en years have elapsed since *The Way of the Goddess* was originally published, and I am as aware of what I *didn't* write as I am of what I did. I was only a few years out of the closet, you see, and the confusion and lack of awareness of a biased public kept me cautious.

Not so now. Now I no longer care to tolerate those opinions. I am what I am, and I am in honorable company relative to the many witches I have initiated since I took high priesthood in 1980.

Two things I would like you to be aware of regarding this work: it was intimated to me over the years by many of my readers that the work displayed a bias toward women. "Not so," say I. It was necessary for me to recount the practices in as personal a genre as possible to forestall it being viewed as a work of dusty authority, and I am, incidentally, a woman. I have amended much of the ritual accordingly, without losing the intent of the content. Secondly, the original work was, as far as I'm concerned, a light work; very much a primer. I have taken this material much further (without dishonoring my sacred oaths), as though I communicate with the students and initiates whom I train.

I do not intend to whitewash the way I know Witchcraft. There is no such thing as a good witch or a bad witch in the common vernacular—one is either very good or training to be so (as opposed to inept). Witchcraft is sorcery, and I understand the term *conscience* by way of its etymological root[2] rather than as it is considered in the current religious sense.

I have included material to familiarize you with the progressive training of the witch in as broad a context as possible without personal contact. I stress that although this manual leans toward the workings of a solitary witch, connection with an established, checked-'em-out-and-they-feel-like-family-ought-to-feel coven is preferable, as the passing-on of initiation, and the one-to-one training that is inherent in a good coven is the surest way of deeply knowing that initiation has taken.

The *Way of the Goddess* was primarily directed to witches of the Southern Hemisphere because, at the time, nothing else did. While sales in the south lands were predictable, those in the Northern Hemisphere were quite vast. I will, therefore, include you more directly in the cross-associations, seasonally, for ease of training.

# INTRODUCTION

All of the techniques described in Part One, Section One are basic requirements for most self-development training in occult traditions. Parts Two and Three are devoted to the rituals and workings of Witchcraft. Whatever you learn is automatically projected into your personal and environmental energy field, and that, in itself, denotes changes not only to your own basic lifestyle, but to the lives of those with whom you associate. You may find yourself with little or nothing in common with people with whom you have consorted for years. You may find yourself in conflict and turmoil, *misunderstood*,[3] and daunted at every turn, unwilling to accept confines to which you may have previously (often unwittingly) acquiesced.

So your challenge is going to be whether or not to break away from your current lifestyle or to somehow incorporate it (and to experiment with the ways to do either). I once knew a woman who had begun training with my coven. She lived with her three children and a husband who had been a part of her life for many years. The children were very understanding but her husband continually harangued her for her newly acquired associates and her involvement in occult practices. There was all kinds of trouble—arguments and walkouts and slammed doors—he would say she had changed and this wasn't the way he expected her to be, and she would refuse to discuss the matter, saying that he didn't want to understand and was jealous of her new-found feelings and teachings.

There were a few of us at my home one night, including this woman, and we talked about her problem (she hadn't invited her husband, he stayed home with the kids). We discussed what *he* believed and what *she* was learning; she also stated that she didn't want to leave her husband. We asked her how certain she was of the ways of magic that she was learning and, because she was determined to continue her training, why she engaged in argument with him at all. She said, "He doesn't want me to follow my path, and I'll be damned if I'll let him interfere!" We asked her how he was interfering and she replied, "He rubbishes me." We asked how, if she was caring about her family and still following the path, his rubbishing could have an effect; that if she really wanted to do it, then he couldn't stop her, and that only through being who she professed to be could she find peace. Sooner or later, if she were loving and laughing and still doing what she knew was right for her, then he would come to accept and appreciate her. This is universally true, for only by living who you really are and what you learn (and not just talking about it) do you ever really grow.

Sometimes, of course, there are real problems associated with being a witch and letting it be known. It would be foolish of me (and untrue) if I denied that you run the risk of losing a whole lot more than just your current thought processes. That is why many of us are publicly silent about our path. The point is that all people have the right to choose how they will live their lives and why not, when we live in a society that does not physically imprison us for attempting to exercise that right? The hardest lesson in your life could be letting go.

Sometimes we take risks that cannot be avoided. The point is to decide for yourself. We do not allow others to assume that they can dictate how we seek and perpetuate truth; start by looking inside yourself for the answers. Whatever your choices, you are ultimately going to affect many people, some of whom you will never meet. The work you do (developmentally and ritually) will change your own life—*always* it will change your own life.

Be aware of whether you are using your trained will to effect these changes[4] or are just playing at training (that will mean trouble!). Many events will occur outside of your conscious control; they occur for good reasons. It is not the incidents themselves that matter, but how you deal with them. Once you have chosen to take upon yourself the obligations of the practice of Witchcraft, then the effects, or the immanence, of this way of life, will be bestowed on you from aligned intelligences, and so will the tests that accompany them.

Anyone who willingly opens themselves to powers beyond the veil of manifestation (as we understand it) opens themselves to the possibility of inner initiation. Witches *know* that they are witches, but initiation is what sets and seals that knowledge through the power of ritual and the intent inherent in the process itself, to a deeper strata of recognition and response both within oneself and from the powers to which we are oathed.

Once initiation has occurred, there is no turning back—you will quest all your life; it is not a thing to do thoughtlessly. Most people's belief[5] structures are conditioned from a very early age by the environmental and socio-cultural norms within which we live. In response to the religious dogma condoned as acceptable by both our parents and peers, we grow up accepting, albeit apathetically, some degree of that dogma, and relate to manifest reality, considerations of deity, and all things termed sacred by the decrees set down by those dogmas. Many people remain consistent with these norms and do not question or pursue them to any depth (I am generalizing).

What is it then that causes some to reject these structures? I guess there are as many reasons as there are people who question, but some reasons stand out more than others. One is anger. Anger has its roots in fear. People who have been taught to fear the wrath of God may become angered at the intensity of this form of manipulation and threat. They will question the fool who would placate them with, "It's the will of God" when a brutal murder by a crazed shooter takes out the life of their schoolmate; they may question the priest who tells the destitute mother of several children that it is wrong to use contraception; they'll question the might of the few to suppress, annihilate, or imprison the many, by whatever justification, for the viewpoint of the many; they'll question the logic of genocide and/or biocide[6] for economic or governmental supremacist ideology; they may question wars fueled by religious divisionist regimes; they may question the right of the cruel and arrogant to prosper above and beyond the loving followers of a pacifist faith. On the one hand, they are being told that "God is love," and on the other they are being told that this same God will cast them into the depths of an eternal fiery hell for any transgressions. If that isn't cause for fear, then I don't know what is. What causes the anger is that the questioner was conditioned into acceptance in the first place.

Then there is that age-old syndrome—curiosity (always with a passion). Curiosity about how other people worship. Curiosity that demands answers that just don't seem to be there in mainstream religions; and when they are given, they often don't make sense. To ask, "Why?" and to be told, "Because it is so" is not what I would call satisfying.

Then there's that other thing! A feeling, a gnawing within the very depths of self that says, "I know Truth, I just haven't found it in my life." Yes! I've heard that one before! There's the breakaway who will not settle for the standards set by others. Not all of them are witches, but all witches know what I mean. It's a not-of-this-life *geas*[7] that shadows the individual through every existence. These people seek their knowledge in unacceptable places. They want to know enough to risk going against the opinions of others, and if they cannot find established groups with whom to share their knowing, then they are quite likely to form their own. They are the illumined individuals who are guided from other realms in their pursuit of Truth, and who are driven to pass on the knowledge gained.

All of these breakaway reasons are valid, and seekers can be found everywhere. The only groups to be wary of, in my experience, are those whose attitudes are hypocritical in practice, or uninformedly critical of others' ways.

Another thing I find unjustified is the need for people to consider God to be in man's image. Why not woman's? Or a bird's? Or even everything all together for that matter? Why is it necessary to give form to something that is supposedly eternal, omnipotent, and vast enough to be capable of creating entire universes? To say that God is like man is to endow God with the qualities of man and to therefore assume that man is supreme (as opposed to what?). This is preposterous, and also too limited! I do consider that the tool, or the vessel, of the imagination is the gateway for the forces that we term divine to express themselves to the individual—that these forces can, and do, mantle themselves in recognizable images to effect communication in recognizable ways. We call these forces, in their divine aspects,

Goddess and God; we name them, synergize with them, dance with them in the way of the sacred, are both at one with them and individual to them, represent them, and revere them, and, in understanding this, weave magic as a matter of course.

Well then, there you are. There are two definite aspects to the work and training of a witch; the first is the discipline of training the magical will through tried and true methods, as shown in Part One. The second, and as important, is the religious training, ritual observances, and spellcrafting techniques that you will find in Parts Two and Three.

As the first section deals wholly with many of the training techniques and understandings that ensure, both magically and analytically, that weakness and ineptitude do not hamper the work side of your chosen path, so the second section deals with the practices of the priest/ess witch. To those of you who can find an authentic coven through which to train, I recommend the process of succession rather than self-initiation. There is nothing that compares with the communion of like souls, welltrained, working the rites of Earth and Sun and Moon and Stars.

# Part One

## THE DISCIPLINES

# Hallowed Be Thy Name

Halled, and walled, with garnet and with topaz
The Temples of my Family!
Deep in scarlet velvet and in black
Come lay with me . . .
Entwine and sweat and softly moan before the Fire;
Beneath the Veil of candles
Lit to show the Way
But slightly, darkly . . .

Unto the music of ghosts;
Unto the ringing of bells within the Shrine . . .

All-hallowed in the rapture
Of the Legend of the Vine
Saved from bleak mortality
By drinking from the Chalice
Of the twice-born; blood turned wine.

. . . and so the Light and Dark were joined for a while; just long
enough for each of Them to remember that their purpose was not
to hate each other, nor disdain each the other . . . but to love each
of the other simply because they were not each other.

Somehow it all got so messed up, so complicated, so confusing;
they were never meant to be enemies . . . whatever gave us that
idea?

—from *The Feast of Flesh & Spirit* by Ly de Angeles

# Section One

# FIRST STAGE TECHNIQUE REQUIREMENTS

## THE CENTER

The center has been called spirit, essence, soul, consciousness. It is the deep you that seeks to know and understand not only who you are, but why you are here. It is the whole of you as opposed to the sum of your parts, it is the gateway to all knowledge, and it is why this book has called to you—like attracts like!

You are aware that you have five senses: taste, touch, smell, hearing, and sight. The aspect of you that is termed the center is the sixth (seventh, eighth, ninth, etc.) sense, or inner sight/sensation. It can best be accessed by considering the other five senses as the perimeter of a circle and all things perceived there flow inward, literally, to the center. The center is also a doorway through which influences not instigated by the conscious mind or from some other source can enter, be assessed, and assimilated into the understanding.

To activate your center consciously (most are already aware of it, but this awareness may not be conscious) it is necessary to consider the center as a watcher. It will use all your five senses to assess not only how you react to others, but how others react to you. It is actively telepathic when you are clear of undisciplined attitudes and "Pavlov's dog" mentality.[8] It will take note of what you are spending your time thinking about and will pass, consciously, just exactly what is valid in terms of what you say, think, and do. It will assess and reassess your reactions to circumstances.

## Exercise

Be aware, before commencing the following, that disciplines are ineffective unless a routine is established because the unconscious is attuned to patterns and will respond easily once the pattern of a conscious routine is rhythmic. Therefore, until each technique is mastered, you will continue with the routine; proficiency is achieved when the pattern is integrated deeply and the technique transforms itself from practice to second nature (at which time the awareness will have become assimilated into who you are and will become an addition to your sixth sense).

Set aside one hour each day and consciously recognize everything you think, do, say, and feel. Imagine that you have an extra set of senses that acts as a camera and recorder, and work at storing all input received during this hour.

Later in the day, claim some quiet time to yourself, recall all the things that you recorded during your designated time, and write them down in an order such as:

- what I saw;

- what I heard;

- what I smelled;

- what I touched;

- what I tasted;

- what I thought about;

- how I was feeling.

This nonjudgmental, external consciousness is called the *Nemet* and is like a beastie that sits on your shoulder. When you have continued with this exercise for several days, you will find that you are automatically doing it all or most of the time. You will be triggering the power of awareness,[9] which will, as a matter of progression, actively trigger latent telepathic and intuitive faculties.

Remember that the center (and its ally, the Nemet) is totally nonjudgmental. It is an observer and a conscious purveyor of how you react and respond within a manifest environment. It will be your task, through your innate understanding of whether you can refine yourself, to act accordingly to whatever the watcher has relayed to you. You may then eliminate or add as you see fit. Take it slowly, as I have seen too many idealists, perfectionists, and impatient people turned into tortured souls, downright bigots, or self-righteous bores through lack of leeway and scope and the ability, like the willow, to bend not only to circumstances, but to ideas and principles that may have been set *for* you and not *by* you!

# Meditation

Meditation is a very ancient technique that has been used worldwide by sages, magi, magicians, witches, wizards, and monks who have taught people who have in turn taught others. The actual word "meditation" is a modern Westernized term for the taming of what could be considered a wild beast—the foreground of one's mind.

There are degrees, or depths, of meditation that you will become aware of the more you practice this technique. If you work on the premise of the circle again (see The Center), then meditation is going within, first to keep within the bounds of that circle, and secondly, to reach the center.

Stop reading for a moment and close your eyes. You will be aware of myriad thoughts and impressions passing through your mindscape. Try this at intervals during the day and behold! it is always the same—constant mental activity. One of the most difficult but necessary means of not only understanding your true nature, but also of *using* the mindscape in practical magic, is through this technique or its variation, contemplation, in a field of either active or passive silence.[10] Otherwise, all you are doing on your quest is accruing more and more external data for your mind to sift, sort, and categorize. This is an addiction inherent in the current collective of the Western seeker—eclecticism ending up being a diffusion of personal power, as the individual who doesn't stay with a Way can never master the tools inherent in the deepening of that Way.

In the day-to-day round of most people's lives, there are constant assaults on the emotions, body, creativity, and intellect. Meditation is the art of halting and transforming these assaults through a positive act of will. The result is not only coping with these assaults, but *riding* them (as opposed to having them ride you) toward a desired outcome with a tranquil mind.

## Meditation and Ritual

It is necessary, within ritual, to be completely clear and centered in order to enable the work to proceed with profundity and intensity. The center is like a doorway to things not currently recognized by the conscious mind. It is your power pack and acts as a lever to not only affect your interactions with the mundane world, but to actualize reception and transmission of information and perceptions from other realms of reality. The process of meditation is like a stimulant that helps your center open and close freely and intentionally and more obviously than before.

## Thought, Telepathy, and the Matrix— The Key to Manifestation

It is advantageous that you realize just what is accessible through this technique. I have spent many years charting and understanding the concept of thought and the body of the mindscape as a way of understanding and tapping into what I was sure was there as a latent or uncontrolled power. I have always been subject to random flashes of telepathy and have traveled the timescape through the use of Tarot to predict future events that *have occurred exactly, explicitly, and, in many, many cases, word for word.* It is not in my nature to leave things that are open to misrepresentation alone until I have an understanding of their pattern, so I experimented with the concept of consciousness to gain a handle on the function.

*What I uncovered is the pattern of thought*—it moves as light moves and is, therefore, instantly there and instantly not. It is both particle and wave, as is light, which, incidentally, is why spells are told to no one. To speak a thing is to collapse the wave, sending the spell into a form of manifestation that may not be material in the observable sense, but is *vibratory*, therefore having presence in material reality. Please think about this! There is both foreground thought and background thought dancing through the mindscape at differing rates of recognizable frequency, and they both exist within a medium; this medium is like space through which both energy and matter realize themselves, but which is a vessel in its own right. Space, both within the mindscape and within recognizable manifest reality, is a *matrix*—and the matrix is the medium through which all things travel. It is a thing of profound silence. It is the spaces *between* thought, and it is through consciously accessing this medium that telepathy and all forms of spellcrafting find their expression. There are no dividing lines here between that which is within and that which is without. Fully realizing this *removes the illusion of separateness* that is the stumbling block to the activation of spellcrafting.

## Exercise

1. Do not do the following exercises in bed until you are used to the technique, as it is likely that you will fall asleep.

2. Have a soft, dim lamp or a lighted candle *behind* you somewhere, as direct or overhead lighting can be very disconcerting.

3. Seat yourself comfortably, either in a straight-backed chair or against a wall, with your hands, legs, and feet uncrossed.

4. Begin (with eyes closed) by taking several deep breaths, filling your lungs to capacity and then exhaling totally. Be aware of breathing by counting your breaths. Take no fewer than ten to begin.

5. Allow your breathing to become natural again.

6.  The aim now is to allow yourself to drift into the velvety-blackness of nonthought. You will initially find that your mind will want to function in overtime; it will trick you into thoughts that seemingly enter your mind of their own volition. Gently, but firmly, push them out again, always aiming for that state of velvety-blackness and nonthought. You can utilize either active or passive silence, understanding that if the active silence tool is music, it should be almost inconsequential, like baroque music played in largo. A similar tool is a metronome set at sixty beats per minute (active silence is of enormous benefit if you have distant sounds of traffic that disrupt you).

7.  Allow just a few minutes the first time, and remember not to apply force against your unwanted thoughts, just gentle pressure. The aim is to still your foreground. Your center is somewhere within that velvety-blackness. When you have reached a state of nonthought, you will have reached your center, which is a state of tranquillity.

8.  Allow yourself to drift there as long as you like or as long as nothing interferes. When you have done this, repeat the deep breathing to rejuvenate yourself, stretch fully, like a cat, and focus on maintaining your sense of tranquillity beyond the exercise.

Continue this process daily, even if only for a few minutes. Give yourself the gift of making time. You are doing three things:

- disciplining your will;

- discovering the sublime silence at the center of your being and activating that center;

- preparing the ground for active and intentional magic.

You will find this technique invaluable when you get down to more specific magical workings, so it is truly desirable to continue practicing and to begin *all* future exercises with the meditative process.

## Contemplation

Contemplation is a very natural way of focusing and inspiring the mindscape. It is best accessed through an activity (sometimes repetitive) that doesn't require the mental concentration of reading or learning (e.g., rocking, watching a fire, simple weaving, unhurried gardening, unhurried cleaning, unhurried, purposeless walking). Contemplation is a time-to-spare active meditation that also gives surcease to foreground mental activity. Out of all of the above, I recommend rocking (preferably in a rocking chair) where no interruption will occur. Issues will arise that require resolution, and in the state of contemplation, they will be resolved. Restraints of consciousness will be recognized in this state; doubts in relation to one's integrity can be addressed here; lies that we perpetuate, or that are perpetuated against us, will come into the full light of awareness. In a state of true contemplation, revelation can also occur, and the space to create change in accordance with these realizations is available.

## Silence

With both of the above techniques, I reiterate, silence is your greatest ally. It is akin to *space*, and it is the mutuality of these two that keeps the gate-between-the-worlds open. It is the bridge between that which is seen and unseen, that which is known and unknown, that which is, and that which is, as yet, unrealized. It is the medium for contact with forces that are drowned out by excess noise and babble. It is aligned with secrecy that is not an elitist function, but a tool of nonadulteration of intent.

# VISUALIZATION

Proficiency at visualization is most important to all occult training. I have encountered only one or two people in all the years that I have been teaching who were unable to visualize. However, they had the ability to conceptualize with similarly accurate results.

The receptacle of the imagination is integral to the processes of creation. Change through intent begins with inspiration, passes through the realm of the imagination, is manipulated by the emotions of enthusiasm, desire, empathy, and compatibility and is transformed into a manifest outcome according to the proficiency of the process (Air, Fire, Water, Earth respectively).

Without the ability to visualize, projection into the astral realms is almost impossible (at least consciously; it is done automatically in the sleep state).[11] The ability to visualize is integral to spellcrafting and can lead to dramatic changes and accomplishments, especially if you are *freefalling*.[12]

The term "visualize" has been described in various ways in many books and by many people. Still, there are some who do not think they can visualize because of *how* it has been described. The problem is one of communication. The word that best articulates the function within the mind that can visualize is *imagination*. To enable me to do justice to this chapter, I would first like to shed light on a common misconception concerning this remarkable power.

Remember the expression used during childhood that related to the bridge between the seen and the unseen? Mum or Dad or some other well-intentioned person would say to you, "Don't be silly, it's just your imagination playing tricks on you," or "You don't see anything there, it was just your imagination." If you were little and the shadow in the corner of the darkened room scared you, it really wasn't much consolation to be told to go back to bed and stop imagining things, was it? *What if there actually had been something there?* Many a natural-born witch, a gifted writer, artist, musician, or inventor may have been deterred from their true path by that demeaning, belittling expression "just your imagination."

Another common distortion of communication that I have heard from teachers of occult, mystical, and metaphysical schools when describing how to visualize is "close your eyes and form the picture behind your closed eyes," and because all there is behind your closed eyes is your closed eyes, you throw up your hands in despair saying, "I can't see anything!"

So visualization *is* the imagination, but not *just* the imagination. Daydreaming without conscious control is probably the closest you could come to the "just . . ." function. The mind is not simply a mechanism that has only one level to its being. There are degrees, or depths, to the imagination that need as much concentrated training as any other technique. When the required depth is plumbed, it is possible to stand with the eyes open and see clearly that which you have created with the power of the mind.[13]

As meditation is the process of stilling the mind while relaxing the body, so visualization utilizes that peaceful, relaxed state for the creation of altered states, increased awareness through controlled and conscious intent, contact, manifestation, and summoning. What begins with the exercise of controlled creation of a one-dimensional image, becomes the creation of a three-dimensional image, then the transmutation of a concept or idea into an image or a series of images, then in turn to the activation of things and people, and the creation of situations that eventually transpire in the realm we understand as material. From there you will seek through the aid of (1) the center, (2) meditation or contemplation, and (3) visualization to transcend the realm of the physical in search of truths that can only be obtained elsewhere.

There are several exercises presented here. You are to train systematically, starting with the first exercise and continuing until you are competent before proceeding to the next. Some of you may find the exercises extremely difficult, while others just sail through. If you are working these techniques in a group venue, please *do not* get competitive. The initial harnessing of the controlled image is the important thing to keep in mind, so *do not* hurry!

## Exercise 1

1. Relax and go into your meditation.

2. Visualize blackness as far as your eyes can see.

3. Onto that black screen, visualize a white circle. Start at twelve o'clock on the circle and visualize eliminating the circle by circumnavigating, clockwise, to where you began. Then recreate the circle the same way.

4. Hold the image of the circle exactly as it is for the count of ten, then eliminate it as before.

*If you lose control of the image for even a moment, do some deep breathing and begin again.* You might not achieve this much in your first few attempts, but continue working at your own pace until you are competent.

## Exercise 2

1.  Begin with Exercise 1 until you have the blackness.

2.  Visualize the circle.

3.  Turn the circle into a sphere and move it around in an attempt to see all of it. Note its texture, size, and color. If it has no color, give it some. Play with it a little. Increase its size, change its substance, etc.

4.  Hold your sphere for as long as you like, and then choose consciously to discontinue. Do not allow stray thoughts to interfere. If they do, begin again or come back to the exercise later.

## Exercise 3

1.  Begin with Exercise 1 until you have the blackness.

2.  Visualize the circle.

3.  Turn the circle into a sphere.

4.  Turn the sphere into a round piece of fruit.

5.  See your own hands holding the fruit. Peel it. Taste it. Chew it. Swallow it, and watch it go all the way down to your stomach (if you do not know your anatomy, look it up; it must be an accurate visualization). Eat the entire fruit following the same procedure. Again, if you have any stray thoughts enter your controlled visualization, stop and either begin again or come back to the exercise later.

Explore an assortment of these image creations when you have mastered the fruit. When you have control of your conscious visualizations, it is time to proceed to the next stage: that of creating a moveable image from an idea or a concept.

## Exercise 4

1.  Begin with meditation in the usual manner.

2.  Choose a concept (e.g., freedom, experimentation, questing).

3.  Contemplate the word to evaluate its meaning for you, both personally and collectively (these concepts need not necessarily be generally accepted).

4.  Visualize the concept by imagining situations or events that justify your evaluation of the concept. Do not lose control of the idea of the exercise and wander into fantasy.

It is advisable not to discuss these later exercises with others. From here you will probably have control of your conscious visualizations, so the next step should be easy. It involves the creation in your imagination of an event that will occur within a set timeframe in your material reality. At this stage, keep things simple and avoid manipulation and egoistical desire-fulfillment events.

## Exercise 5

Create, by use of the technique of controlled visualization, an event, featuring people with whom you are in fairly regular contact, in which certain key phenomenon are brought to bear. Keep it concise, but ascertain that what you summon into actuality is not a common occurrence, such as saying hello to George down the street on your way to work as you always do. Keep it snappy and distinct, and keep a written record. Place your event within limited time coordinates (e.g., within one week from the day it was visualized.)

As you may have gleaned by now, not only does this technique require control and have, inherently, limitless possibilities, it also demands a certain ethic. Be aware that even though you can utilize this technique within the realms of manifestation, you will ultimately bear the consequences. The Law of Congruity,[14] of cause and effect, should be contemplated.

# Section Two

# NEVER TO WALK IN ANYONE'S SHADOW

## SELF-ANALYSIS TECHNIQUES

The biological animal and the soul that infuses it has an innate ability to handle its own life and transcend both the internal and the external problems that arise through merely being alive (in this time, within certain conditions). I will begin this section by throwing into the ring a particular word that is crucial in the category of detriment: *conditioning*. The majority of dysfunctions that arise and entrench themselves in our lives are caused because of preconditioned expectations and assumptions.[15]

Have a good honest look at your life as it is right now: the people, things, and events around you, the way they affect you, how you react or respond to them, what you think about when thinking about the individuals who are close and not so close to you, and about those who pepper your life. How much time do you spend dwelling on past events? How much time is spent speculating on the future? There! Hours of time!

People relinquish ownership of their lives to others so quickly (especially where love is concerned) that the responsibility for what happens to us relative to knowing those people automatically falls on them as if we had no control. Take, for example, the commonly used expressions, "Look what you are doing to me!" or "It's all your fault!"

Why? When did it transpire that another ordinary person was given the power over your life to such a degree? *Whatever happened to freedom of choice?* Everyone has the power to change their living arrangements if they are threatened or disempowered by what is happening to them. To lay the blame of one's own inadequacy of responsibility on someone else and expect them to comply is to deny both you and them the right to a mind, a spirit, and the pleasure of living.

For a witch, it is unacceptable! An occultist cannot afford to place the control of his or her life in the hands of anyone or anything else, and as I have already made abundantly clear, the control of your will is the focal point of training.

## Exercise 1

1. Choose a quiet place where you will not be interrupted. If you are working the technique alone, you will need pencil and paper. If you are working with someone else, they will need the pencil and paper. They will question you and record the replies.

2. Write at the top of one side of the page, **What I Want.** Under that, write the numbers one through twenty down the page.

3. Write at the top of the other side of the page, **What I Need.**

4. Fill in all twenty lines of the first side with anything you want. *Be honest with yourself.* Say the things aloud as you write, and list twenty things (you can write more, not fewer).

5. When you have completed side one, turn the page over and write twenty or more things you need. Write until you have exhausted your answers.

6. Now compare your two lists.

7. Take another piece of paper and write at the top, **Why?** Go ahead and ask yourself, honestly, why you want what you want. Then do the same, on the other side of the paper, for your list of needs.

Contemplate, for all answers, what would really happen to you if you didn't get what you want or need, and what you would really feel if you did (some people I have worked with have included in their "need" list things they already have—pay attention to the question).

Gauge for yourself how important these things are to your well-being. If they really are not that necessary, then *clear them from your mind* because they are excess baggage, but if you could fill in twenty lines in the first place, then the excess was already there and your self-esteem would have been consistent with it.

Advertising, concepts of what is deemed successful, and concepts of what is deemed acceptable are all effective means of manipulating the individuality of a person or a people into conformist models. It's okay to do what you do because you want to, and sometimes it's a matter of necessity to don the mask, but it's honorable to *know* who you are within the whole of it all and to don the mask only when it is expedient to do so—*never forgetting that it's a mask!*

## Exercise 2

This exercise makes use of what is called the *Book of Elements.* It's going to be one of your primary grimoires. The technique is commonly used by most of the occultists whom I have known (myself included), and it works on the premise that practitioners will consistently work at erasing any mundane conditioning complexes that inhibit their ability to concentrate on, and control, whatever they do within their Craft.

The self (the circle) is divided into four somewhat equal parts (I say somewhat because although they are, in essence, equal, it is usually the case that the section dealing with emotions takes the most practice to balance.)

The four parts are Fire, Water, Earth, and Air. The *qualities* of these elements are as variable as the manifest elements themselves, so I prefer to present the manifest expressions prior to relating them to personality expressions.

## Manifest Expressions

### Fire

- Flame (all—from the flame of a candle through hearth fire to raging, out-of-control forest fires)
- Electricity
- Fission
- Friction
- Combustion
- Light
- Brilliance
- Heat
- Transformation through interaction with other elements

### Water

- Lakes, rivers, oceans, dew, rain
- Aqueous bodily secretions
- Moisture (condensation, dampness, steam)
- Wetness
- Liquid
- Nonconforming limitlessness
- Mutability
- Magnetism
- Transformation through interaction with other elements

**Earth**

- All things solid

- That which is tactile

- Tangible reality

- Subject to the transformative function of decomposition

- Ground; both in its electrical sense and in its relativity to that which supports life (as we understand it)

- Structure and form

- Dimension

- Time

- Existence (as a sensate phenomenon)

- Transformation through interaction with other elements

**Air**

- All things atmospheric

- Gases

- Space

- That which is celestial

- Theory

- That which is ethereal or etheric

- Frequency

- Noumenon

- Sound and the medium through which it travels

- That which is invisible

## Personal Expressions

### Fire

People display the qualities of Fire when they are:

- Spontaneous

- Optimistic

- Lusty

- Impetuous

- Blatant

- Outspoken

- Demonstrative

- Combustible

- Ruthless

The qualities of creativity, self-expression through the spoken and written word, enthusiasm, aggression, and, often, boisterousness are demonstrations of a Fire-dominant individual.

### Water

People display the qualities of Water when they are:

- Artistic

- Empathic

- Passive

- Feeling

- Sensual

- Confused

- Unpredictable

- Dreamy

- Indecisive

- Doubtful

- Inscrutable

- Enigmatic

- Romantic

The qualities of intuitiveness, inventiveness, responsiveness, nurturing, and the use of innuendo, self-pity, and victim-consciousness because of a lack of personal boundaries are demonstrations of a Water-dominant personality.

**Earth**
People display the qualities of Earth when they are:

- Productive

- Precise

- Calculating

- Sexual

- Determined

- Stubborn

- Aesthetic

- Petty

- Belligerent

- Brave

- Predictable

The qualities of perseverance, administration, fixety, strategy, and orthodoxy are demonstrations of the Earth-dominant personality.

**Air**

People display the qualities of Air when they are:

- Changeable

- Inspirational

- Logical

- Intellectual

- Idiosyncratic

- Exacting

- Unpredictable

- Challenging

- Abrasive

- Solitary

- Musically inclined

- Expansive

- Explicit

- Technical

- Scientific

The qualities of rhythm and harmony, quick-temperedness, rigidity, and the tendencies to analyze, get caught in the past, and to display either too much emotion or be unable to express emotion are all demonstrations of the Air-dominant personality.

To work the *Book of Elements*, you will first need to purchase a notebook and divide it into four equal parts. Title the first section Fire, the second section Water, the third Earth, and the fourth Air. Divide the pages of each section into two equal columns, one side titled Acceptable and the other titled Unacceptable. Down each side, list your own qualities and habits relative to those headings.

This is a process of self-observation, and it quite often takes several weeks or months, as you will not be aware of many of your traits without accompanying experiences to trigger them. Once you are finished with your lists, look over the attributes of Earth, Fire, and Air and determine how many so-called unacceptable self-judgments are actually Water- or emotion-based. Rearrange accordingly.

Then decide how many, or which, of the unacceptable aspects of yourself are socio-culturally inclined (i.e., conditioned by your upbringing), and adjust your opinion according to your own standards, based on determining ethics, and which of those attributes can be eradicated or transmuted into more comfortable alternatives.

Consider two things:

1.  Witchcraft is a way of life for individuals, not the masses, and there's no point in you coming toward the Craft if you are a wimp, a follower, a coward, or a fool, as sorcery is both a practice and a priesthood, and it is not a garment that can be discarded when the going gets tough. The main emphasis of the above technique is to understand your own nature well enough to *get clear of fear* based on speculation rather than actuality (we will cover fear later in this section) and to weave your webs accordingly.

2.  Your aim is to get to the center of yourself and your motivations, and to find the big issues that undermine your capacity to respond in true will, after first having eradicated the blinds to those big issues (e.g., self-justification based on the opinions of others).

When you have completed your *Book of Elements* and have gone over it and over it to see if you can add or subtract anything, I suggest you *get rid of it!*

As long as you allow yourself to be conditioned to entertain the expectations of others, as long as you allow yourself to wallow in a lack of control and self-respect, as long as you allows others to direct the states of your emotional and physical well-being, you are unable to truly develop any abilities of a psychic or occult nature, as you will be constantly living in some state of anticipation or stress, under pressure from yourself. In this state, you are ever seeking to please others for their attention or seeking to dominate them for fear of "Not."

## *Mulengro*

I know your Name now, you Liar!

You, the killing machine of the soul!

I'll tell!

I'll tell!

If they can hear me they will know your Name also!

Too late! You are known: "Divide and Conquer"!

YOU ARE THE LIE THAT CLOSES OFF THE GATE!!

Your Faces, they are 7!

Your essences, they are 7!

Your Powers, they are 7!

And together they are you! Mulengro!


You are Greed!

You are Envy!

You are Guilt!

You are Deceit!

You are Denial!

You are Expectation!!

You are Assumption!!

—from *The Feast of Flesh & Spirit* by Ly de Angeles

## Mulengro

*Mulengro* is the name of an entity that is like an alien barb; one that has become an out-of-control arrow that pierces generation upon generation with its poison. It feeds on its own likeness, and people are its host. Mulengro could be considered to be like the Qliphoth of Qabbalah and the devil that Christianity invented in the Middle Ages to ensure obedience to its dogma.

Certain regimes utilize Mulengro's force as a tool of manipulation. In Machiavelli's work of the fifteenth and sixteenth centuries, he outlines the strategy (in his infamous book *The Prince*) of getting and keeping political power over a people based on the principle of divide and conquer. I cite Machiavelli as he is synonymous with Mulengro, and his tools of manipulation are still taught today.

Mulengro denies the individual the right to be an individual and assures that its victims remain emotionally crippled. Mulengro is passed on like a virus through the perpetuation of the seven attributes of greed, envy, guilt, deceit, denial, expectation, and assumption. The only way of ridding the psyche and the spirit of the virus is to abruptly and completely stop hosting it!

Do not allow others to perpetuate any of the these seven faces of Mulengro on you, and do not use them to abort the truth, no matter what the seeming advantage. These faces (behind each of them are the other six) are all vices of disrespect.

How are you to know what is really true or false when Mulengro clouds your vision? It is like a voracious weed seeking to smother a mother forest. I warn you that the eradication of these acceptable modes of behavior will place you squarely outside of the general flow of the social stratum. That's okay. The Way of a witch is not for everyone.

## NOTES ON HUMAN NATURE

The most important aspect of a well-trained initiate is the acquisition of balance. There are four sides to the nature of people:

1. The bright, laughing, joyous side, the side we have been taught in our culture to honor and to seek to show the world; the side that is at peace and is not fulfilled.

2. The quester; the one that seeks to change what is immediately perceived as limiting. This side of people's nature is concerned with what is on the outside. It is the side that seeks to imprint one's very existence on both other people and our environment (it seeks the relevance of immortality), and it is not fulfilled.

3. The third side is all mixed up with learning and patterns, understanding, creativity, and curiosity. It is a very brave side, but it is not fulfilled.

4. The dark side? The hidden one? In our culture, because of Mulengro, we are taught this side is wrong and should be suppressed, destroyed, that it is evil and dangerous. We are taught to seek to fulfill the other three (to be nice!) and to deny the fourth, and, as a consequence, it becomes a dragon within the self! All our pain, both physical and emotional, all our dead ends, our unresolved angers and resentments, all our futilities pour down the tunnel of the psyche to the individual underworlds of each of us—and stay there! The person who has not been touched by hurt is not lucky, they are defenseless or they are lying.

*This is our wild side!* As those who have known pain will tell you, it is the most powerful side, as within it resides not only all our experiences, but our racial and instinctual memories, our attachment to the collective unconscious, our ability to perpetuate the first three on the list, to transcend considered limitations, to survive—even our will to live. Within it resides our ability to protect as well as to procreate and perpetuate, our sense of union with our planet and with those things on our planet that have not yet been subdued, tamed, or destroyed, and our ability to work sympathetic magic.

This side is like a wild horse. There are different ways to coerce it to become ridable. Brutality is certainly one way (but what about the horse's spirit!). Empathy, firmness, and patience are another way—a way that ensures a different kind of mount. All of the techniques in Part One are about establishing the bond between horse and rider.

## Fear

I have a wonderful etymological dictionary that often assists me in understanding manners of communication at a deeper level than is acceptable in the common vernacular. I read my first dictionary, like a paperback novel, when I was twelve years old because I'd won it in a *Book Week* competition at school and thought it was the correct thing to do with a new book. There's power in words. Oral communication is like a gift from the gods or one's worst nightmare, depending on its application.

My dictionary informs me that the word "fear" comes from the Old English word *faer*, which is related to the word *faerie* and means to cast enchantments. Faerie, or fairy, has roots in the word *fae* or *fay*, meaning of the Fates, or fate, which, in turn, is linked to faith, derived from the Latin word meaning *to trust*.

Yeah, yeah, yeah, you might say; however, I leaped into the whole fear concept several years ago because I was hearing so many people use the word often and so commonly: "I'm afraid this will happen," "I'm afraid to think," "I'm afraid things haven't turned out," "I'm afraid of what I'd do if I didn't have this job." Even, and perhaps more aptly, "I'm afraid for my life!"

From this I calculated that fear is about *not having*, and it rises up into consciousness when one is not ready, or prepared in some way, for certain expected or anticipated eventualities. Fear always seems to be of what's *out there* or *unknown*, but I heard much that was irrational, and so I looked to myself in this matter.

I am a particularly resilient witch and put much of that down to one of the first philosophies I was ever taught by one of the women in my family, which was "Fix it or forget it!" If you can't fix it, then let it go! If I am staring down the muzzle of a tiger, it is easier to relax than to fight the inevitable. The fight or flight syndrome, which describes the physiological symptom of threat, leaves out *freeze*, which is what fear is also about. The freeze instinct is important and should not be misrepresented. Being a witch, I summoned Fear as an entity, and *he was beautiful!*

He appeared, when I first summoned him, tall and stooped, big, hooded, and draped in mists and swathes of gray, from pale to almost black. There was a line between him and me. He walked over the line and stood just behind my left shoulder. He's there now. He stoops and whispers in my ear, "Watch out!" "Don't trust what you're hearing," "Slow the car down," "Trust the omens!" He is Fear. He warns me of probable danger, and I listen to him because he is always correct.

Fear is your ally! It is your instinct to survive. Worry is a useless thing; it achieves nothing. Resolution is the key to distress.

## *Elohim Gibor No. 3*

I saw a black jaguar lope towards me and sit.


I have no compassion—I am instinct.

I sense EVERYTHING! and all is there to regard or disregard.

Let the river run unaided,

let the mountain stand untended,

let the temple stand within the jungle lost to those who

seek their answers in the now.

The snow-leopard hunts in silent white,

the eagle waits on silent wings—

the watcher is and does in silence.

Shhhhh . . .

the silent hunt awaits the majesty of the kill—

instinct, focus, silence—

all are preparations!

Keep low upon the ground and let the wind work with you;

it's worth the wait if you seize it!

There is power in the wait when the waiting is no more—

it depends on whether you are ready!

—from *The Feast of Flesh & Spirit* by Ly de Angeles

# THE ETHICS OF PERSONAL POWER

The lifescape of magic and Witchcraft is a *place* and a *way* of being rather than the paradigm of *something one does*. We know each other by recognizing the way in which we live and that which is within each of us that has lived, thus, forever. It is the recognition of the *quest*.

The nature of initiation will keep you questing for the rest of your life. There will be no surcease. There is no walking away from this once it has called your name and you have *willingly* answered. The forces that you work with will continue to feed and inspire you; and everything ends up being looked at through eyes that know how to see.

Like attracts like is also a certainty. You will come into contact with others of the Craft with whom you can share and synthesize. These like-minded individuals can become an important focus for honor and truth, and they will be powerful allies should the need arise. It is most important that you establish ethics at the onset of your relationships so that honor is not betrayed later. The ability to abuse the forces with which one is aligned has been perpetrated before, and the ego is always responsible. This could be considered a conditioned response, as we are brought up in a society that promotes competition and aggressive striving for sometimes superfluous success—the seeking of power for its own sake being one of the false reasons for accessing this quest. This is an identity-seeking excuse for lots of people. Their desire to access the landscape is, itself, valid. They often have the feeling without the knowing to mirror themselves. I am writing this manual mainly for them.

Some people will seek, accumulate information, and call it knowledge. They seek it for the sake of owning, possessing it to access an identity, and they end up with exactly nothing. The reason for the seeking of knowledge, and the practical application of it, is to *become* that which your soul knows you are, by your very nature, and to be a vessel for this knowledge to create change in accordance with the pattern inherent in magic and mysticism. It is unnecessary, for example, to acquire the fanciest ritual regalia, to wear the fanciest of robes, to drape oneself in all the appropriate jewelry. When people set out to accumulate for the sake of how impressive they appear, others of the Craft become wary of the reasons this is being done. The art of one's ritual things is, however, greatly respected.

Remember that quantity is not relative to quality in the occult arts and sciences. Your prime expression comes from *who* you are, the *direction* of your learning, and the *application* of knowledge, understanding, and wisdom.

## AWARENESS

Don't miss anything. In all of your undertakings, have all your senses working at their fullest potency; this is necessary in your magical, ritual, and personal activities. Of primary significance is the activity of your sixth sense, which will have been triggered/awakened by the preceding exercises, and which will pick up the exchanges of energy in interactive circumstances.

You will hear more in a conversation if you truly listen; you will see more going on around you if your observation entails more than simply looking. There is a leap that is actualized through exercising trust in your own cognitive ability to understand how interactive energy is used in either honorable or manipulative ways.

Awareness is the activation of the Nemet.

Awareness is the ability to literally read the feeling in the air.

Awareness means control of one's undertakings.

## PREPARATION

The preparation required of you when working magic, as well as ritual, is to be done with the idea of excellence kept clearly at the forefront of your thoughts. Should you be preparing a sacred space in which to work magic and ritual, seek to personalize the entire process by doing the best you can.

As your awareness assists you in being prepared for whatever you are doing, or for the next stage of your quest, so preparation is a necessary function of intent.

# Intent

Know, at all times, *why* you are doing what you are doing. Know your own motives well. Exercise caution in your undertakings, as each action, each thought, is to be clearly of your own choosing. Each thought and every action will engender, progressively, a response relative to it *for which you are solely responsible.* I say progressively because you will become aware, in this manner, of a deepening of self as the illusions drop from you like a snake shedding an outmoded skin.

There is no reason to set up a ritual circle or cleanse with intent of purification unless there is an *intent.* That intent can be as simple as seeking contemplation as a passive form of ritual, or as complex as the experiment of a Qabbalistic Mass in the tradition of the Golden Dawn. It matters not if your intent is unclear. The lack of intent will reflect on the evolving whole, as each initiate has an effect, like the butterfly effect in the chaos theory.

# Focus

Focus is rather difficult to describe in a linear fashion. It is achieved when you link emotion and intellect in one function for the purpose of actualization, by will, of a desired outcome. It does not allow the ego to interfere with its function. It is the deep stillness. It is the silence behind all action/interaction. It does not allow the mind or the heart to act independently of the purpose it seeks to attain.

## PERSONAL POWER

Personal power is a *natural growth process* that develops as a result of the life you live in the way of the witch. Others will notice you even when you do not desire to be noticed;[16] therefore, personal power is the ability to disappear when you want to and appear when you want to. It is *not* an egoistical phenomenon! It is an energy (akin to magnetism), a presence about oneself that will require a firm rein for the first few years. It will emanate from your physical body like a field phenomenon. *This field is neither a conscious, nor consciously acquired, function,* and you are to know and understand this. Posturing and arrogance are its illusory counterparts. Personal power should not be treated as such (that will be the ego seeking to manipulate a natural force and *that* is both ugly and offensive).

Personal power is a *direct* result of accessing the lifescape of magic and of living within its field. If you allow yourself to become glamoured[17] by it, in either yourself or anyone else, you disrupt the web of the worlds and the places of power will withdraw, oh, even just a little, from the access of those who seek to live within their wonder.

Personal power is an accumulation of awareness, preparation, intent, and your ability to focus, all through the vessel of the self.

## SERVICE

Let's not confuse the word *service* with the word *servitude*. You service the forces with which you interrelate. You are in service to life itself. This is our deity, which we consider both our Goddess and our God.

This is Witchcraft at the core.

Your service is to the truth of that which you perpetuate and the need to be on call when you are moved by the intelligence of these forces. Nothing is required beyond the truth, and while the truth may be exceedingly confrontational to either you or another, it does not engender harm. You will strive to dispel unwarranted fear by reaching beyond the face of fear to seek its source.

It is knowledge and understanding of ourselves *at the very source* that is contacted through confrontation with adversity (the dark faces of Goddess and God). To know and understand what it is that engenders fear enables us to penetrate and address perceived inadequacies where possible, hence to grow beyond what we thought we were. You will seek to remain unattached to the outcomes of your endeavors, knowing that the above has been understood; for to do other would be to become entrapped in a place of resentment, blame, or rejection (want).

You may have fixed concepts about what you believe will provide happiness, and this may be a false focus. You will trust that the thrust of your destiny, which places you in a situation you don't consciously want to be in, is leading you on your quest. At all times, when these events occur, you will seek to understand why without necessarily comprehending the entirety of the process, as this will, in retrospect, become obvious in its patterning. You will most certainly consider the phrase "your gods will not barter," because they won't—no matter how you moan. Personal gain may not come to you in material form; that is a limited ideology of wealth—the universe does not necessarily consider the need for payment for services rendered in recognizable goods.

Know the Law of Congruity! Understanding yourself is the first key; seeking to reconcile seeming opposites is the second key; coming to know that, and how, magic works is the third key.

## THE LAW OF CONGRUITY

The Law of Congruity is the law of cause and effect: every action has an equal and opposite reaction. That does *not* imply that the effect is either relative or recognizable in any human evaluation—it simply is what it says it is. The Law of Congruity does not apply to matter only, but to thought and energy (such as speech and mood). The Eastern term for this law is called karma, and it is balanced by dharma, the recognition of the law of karma (which is like fate or destiny) that allows the balancing of imbalance through right speech, thought, and action.

All of our techniques so far have been for the purposes of control and clarity *without* force. All of the techniques so far have aimed at opening you up to the reality of the Law of Congruity. The point here is that you now know how to redress dysfunctions so that your magic is untainted by ineptitude and your priesthood in Witchcraft is clear of false images. You know now. Once you know a thing, you can't *unknow* it.

Once you know a thing, any deviation from the truth of that knowing will go crashing out of control, not only through your own consciousness, but out into the world of manifestation, much, much louder than it would have been before you knew, therefore arcing back to you the experiences relative to the harmonic of that dysfunction. Do you see now? The clearer you get, the louder the clang of any deviation from that clarity—that's the Law of Congruity. So, also, is the harmonic of clear, focused will when it travels from you, ensuring that the return arc is synchronistic. That's spellcrafting at its maximum effectiveness.

The Law of Congruity: every action has an equal and opposite reaction. Please contemplate this. It is the foundation of successful spellcrafting.

# On Passion

Hard core? Austere? The works written for you, thus far, are the training requirements that I have been through, and each initiate that I have trained has been through, in their own way and in their own time. I don't want you to misunderstand. This is not a recipe for an ascetic, because *that's not Witchcraft!* Austerity is not the way of the Craft, *ever!* The trainings are there to help you become clear, to allow your brightness and purpose to be absolutely awakened along with any and all latent psychic talents; but it takes art to keep the balance.

I tend to move from wild, passionate moods to deep introspection, from frivolity to icy-coldness toward others, from the desire to be exact and exacting in the implementation of my rituals (both with and without the coven) to wanton abandonment. I've learned that to be really alive is to be like the weather, like the ways of the Earth. I am prone to making lists, to perpetuating habits and routines, so I break them when I feel so inclined to remember to be spontaneous.

I am sensual, calculating, theatrical, isolationist, and social, tired, overworked, restless, and lazy—but clear! I know why I do what I do, even when driven by passions that can't always be interpreted as rational. I am capable of handling the consequences of living on the edge—loving men I can't have and men I can, not wanting anyone to ever tell me what I should or shouldn't do!

I am *experimential* (my word), cautious, unwilling to accept limitations. Witchcraft is all about living to the heights and depths of life as a *way of worship*. So do the work, but keep alive the wonder or you'll end up being bored; you'll end up being old when a witch, like the Earth, can be both immeasurably ancient and ever-young! Don't be bothered by a roll in the dirt once in a while, or a tendency to fall in love—that's the Way of the Goddess!

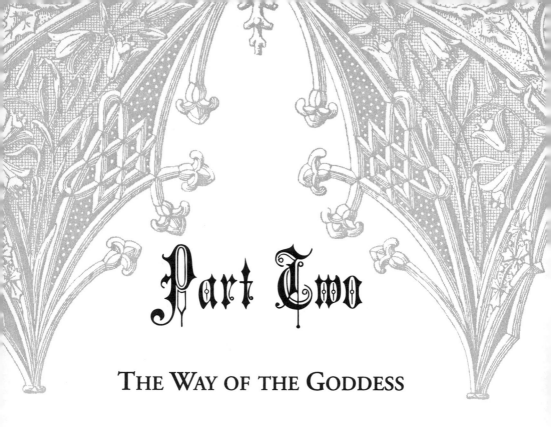

# Part Two

## THE WAY OF THE GODDESS

## *Geburah*

I am Power . . . beyond anything you can imagine!
Mine are the eagle and the tiger.

You battle the Elements and life . . .

Why!!!

Suppress anxiety; Overcome the "tragedy"—
Take both your hands and hold them up and cry
Freedom!

. . . then walk the paths offered to you.

> The Warrior is the weapon,
> *Not* the weapon in the hands of
> the Warrior!

—from *The Feast of Flesh & Spirit* by Ly de Angeles

## Section One

# REQUIRED UNDERSTANDING
# PREPARATORY TO THE
# PRACTICE OF RITUAL

## TO BE WITCH

We are a priesthood that works specific rituals for specific purposes, and sorcery (magic) because we have the ability, through our trainings, to do so. A witch is either a woman (most often) or a man (in certain traditions called a warlock—I've no problem with that) who *knows* that he or she is a witch. A true witch is a *natural*. I've never yet met a true witch who felt like something else. I've met a lot of people who want to *be* witches, who dress and talk the part, but when you're not, you're not.

A witch realizes certain powers; represents, rather than worships them; calls them Goddess and God (without it being a fixed, or boxed, ideology) and invokes them; fuses with them, emotes, and lives them; recognizes them in the vast forces of nature and beyond that (within other frames of reference).

Witches are priestesses or priests, initiates to these powers, and are never laity. They are secretive in their undertakings and do not proselytize. Certain of us work with the publishing trade to reach others of our kind and also to dispel the ignorance that has, at certain times, arisen to cause harm to those who walk a different way than that which is considered orthodox.

There's no such thing as a good, or white, witch. There's no such thing as a bad, or black, witch. There is only an admirable shade of gray, as each witch is answerable only to those powers to which he or she is oathed and to the axiom "Do as ye will e'er it harm none," which is the only tenet to which we adhere. The phrase has become flippant as a result of its widespread usage within both the neo-pagan and the neo-witch movements of the late twentieth century to the point where I have heard it used as an excuse for nonaction in the face of necessary responsibility, and so we will examine it here.

Many of the ways of working magic will be described for you in the following sections of this manual. They are things you will want to know about at some time or other, whether the need to use them arises or not. Although I will provide you with many techniques, the ability to work them will be dependent on who you are and whether you *are* a witch (based on the definitions above).

Two common expressions associated with what constitutes a witch that are both absolutely true: "A witch is born, not made," and "It takes a witch to make a witch."

1.  It's in the blood, no matter how many generations it may not have been acknowledged (and self-preservation may very well have been why seven or ten or fifteen or more generations ago your ancestor shut up about it and did not pass the knowledge down the line). Like a dormant seed, it waits until the season is fertile for it to germinate.

2.  Unless the witch is willing to take initiation when the magic calls, and to actively, consciously, and with free will, walk across the line to live *in* the world but not *of* it, and to take the oaths of priesthood, then the line is not crossed. The power will withdraw because it knows the witch is not ready. "Some other time," it seems to say. That's okay, too, understand, because you won't be the same as everyone else. Even the vernacular of witches, when they gather, is either hooded or inscrutable to cowans (the term for people who are not witches—it's an insider word and not an elitist one!).

    Witches work sacred ritual to Earth and Moon and Sun and Star (these are covered in this section and the next) as an outcome of the priesthood and as a means of removing the barriers of separateness that are the current blindness of our species. As a way of keeping the powers strong within our pattern as a people of the Earth, the pattern is of the cycles of the seasons of Earth and Moon and Sun and Star. It is also our responsibility to develop our deeper talents (each to their own) of psychic capacity and the ability to cast enchantments; to study and come to know and understand the ways of the sacred of other people; to constantly strive to broaden our capacity to learn in whatever areas life presents to us and in whatever areas we choose; to treat the whole bloody thing as the art that living most assuredly is, and to perpetuate and project that art as the gifts we can give to life.

## Do As Ye Will, E'er it Harm None

The term "harm" is perpetrated through either ignorance or intent. Ignorance is a social problem brought about because the flesh we eat is prepackaged and is often not considered flesh; because our fruit and vegetables are all stacked on the shelves at the local shop and other foods are boxed or jarred or tinned or wrapped in neat containers that very often give no hint of their having lived at all; because at some time or other hunting became product distribution and disassociation, and separation became acceptable. It's all a lie, isn't it? Absolutely *everything* we consume was killed to feed us. Mass producers of trendy foods appeal to the hedonist in people. They use trickery to coerce the public into believing their products are "good for them" or are somehow socially impressive. The ease of fast foods is a trickery that caters to the idea of affluence, creating a false sense of detachment to the whole life-and-death process.

Intent, relative to harm, is all about cowardice, as Oscar Wilde said in *The Ballad of Reading Gaol* when he wrote,

> Yet each man kills the thing he loves,
> By each let this be heard,
> Some do it with a bitter look,
> Some with a flattering word.
> The coward does it with a kiss,
> The brave man with a sword!

The person who lies creates disillusionment and perpetuates the closed door of their victims' intuition and ability to live safely, and knows what he or she is doing. The person who mutilates a garden or a forest for greed and with an "I'm all right, Jack, and that's all that matters!" attitude knows what he or she is doing. The person who does not consider the repercussions of their actions (this also applies to a society or a culture) knows what he or she is doing. An institutional or authoritative body that tells us how to live and threatens or humiliates those who do otherwise (either by choice or circumstance), and a society that has come to expect our government and judicial system to lie and to perpetuate preferentialism is as responsible as the system that perpetuates the dysfunction, because "to acquiesce is to condone" (John F. Kennedy).

To be awake to what you do and to do it without denial, is to honor the interwoven dance of life and death, the certainty of change, your right to choose, and a clear awareness based on the principles of your priesthood, of how you approach, act, and resolve each and every event and issue.

# *The Beginning*

*We stood upon the shore of a great sea. We looked out to the horizon from whence we had come with a longing so painful that none of us could talk about how we felt. Lost upon the shore of an unknown land in the night of a new age with none but ourselves to call upon as friends.*

*We had been warned; the Oracle had gathered those of us who now stand here and had told us that the Sun had taken toll of the great Crystal and that all was finished. An end to our lands must surely come and the voice of the stars had said, "Go!"*

*So we took to our boats with nothing but that which we treasured, our Knowledge, our Names and our Inheritance.*

*Now the Plain lies behind us, lit by strong moonlight. It beckons us to begin the voyage of timeless restoration and so we turn from the longing and the remembering and, one and all, Priest and Priestess alike, set out to fulfill that which had been foretold.*

*We stand, now, among the Great Stones, and seek through our rites to the Moon and Sun to bring peace to this ravaged land. The Great Stones shine as once did the Crystal, and the answer comes to the Oracle that much will change but that the seeds of our past shall reach into the distance of time. Further, it is said that what we know will not die but will be carried within the being of the children of our race, who will be born again and again and again . . .*

—Ly de Angeles

# Goddess and God of My Priesthood

To be able to present this subject at all has taken me years of deep introspection and, currently, days of figuring out how to tell you without pretension, without resorting to easy answers, as easy answers are far too common. I have been involved, with others of my kind, in a quest for several years now, a quest concerned with the true nature of communication. There's power in communication—to talk when there's something to say, and not for the sake of just hearing oneself, to say what is said without lying, generalizing, or profaning the art. The experiment of both speaking and *thinking*, as well as evaluating, in this manner clears away vast misconceptions, trivia, and dross, and creates a psychic, spiritual, emotional, and intellectual ability to understand things at a profound level and, therefore, to live within the landscape of magic as a clear vessel of that which we, as initiates, represent.

Through communion with the bipolar nature that we call Goddess and God, we align with their immanence to consequentially realign that which is at variance to their pattern. We now understand this: that it is not what one feels one should be doing or should not; not what one might be or might not; not what is termed right or wrong, but *who* one is, as well as what one does, that engenders change—that is the magic! Because so much of who we are is connected to a philological perspective (even, and especially, pertaining to consciousness and conceptual religion), it is by drinking from the wellspring of clear communication that the intelligence of an individual is aligned with the sacred.

It is by the intentional use of certain words that I seek to have you know how *I* know of Goddess and God, and thence, how they are understood at a cultural level. To simply rattle off the considered phrases associated with this force is where I let others down in the original publication of this work. I want to talk this book *to* you, not *at* you; to have you understand that everything is personal and we all get to the point where dry rote authoritative texts are just plain babble.

## Exercise for the Purpose of Clear Understanding

To comprehend the next phase of writing, I ask that you look up each pertinent word in the following text for its etymological significance rather than simply reading it quickly, as the contemplation of the idea behind certain words opens one up to the entity or the genii of that word. It's somewhat of a Pandora's Box at times, but profound for all that!

So, how does one define something infinite? The Goddess is ineffable, inscrutable, immense, immanent, indivisible, profound; yet She is explicit in the projection of Her nature into the consciousness of either an individual or a people, personal in Her mutuality. She is that-which-is and, as such, there is nothing that is not Her! All Her brothers, lovers, sons are the expressions of our God. Behind their many names is one force that expresses itself in many ways for the love of itself in its own diversity (divided for love's sake on the chance of union). She is the chain reaction of time's expression, but She is not time. Life is Her setting for the eternal dance of transformation, hence the cycles and the seasons of everything from personal experience to galaxies. She dances with God in a dance of love and hate, elation and tragedy, death and resurrection, destruction and rejuvenation because they are not simply life, *but the experience of living!*

Their offspring are eternally themselves, everbecoming; and though all things have the appearance of being progressive, separate, and divisible, She is all things. That's why She is also known to be a mystery; that's why Her mysteries are of the Moon, of space, of the Underworld; that's why one of Her mirrors is the sea and why another is the Earth and why life even *is* at all.

Progenitor, matrix. We think of Her only as "She," but the very fact that we *do* think of Her as "She" informs us that that's the way She *wants* to be known to us as a people. What is it that makes a woman a woman? With or without a womb, with or without having made children, fertile or infertile, there is a quality inherent in the creation and continuum of woman that is Hers alone, just as there is a quality inherent in man that can never be of woman. I *refuse* to profess to define it! Therefore, within us, as a species, woman expresses Goddess (whether consciously or not) and man expresses God (whether consciously or not) and within them both, as with Goddess and God, resides the other—right down to the DNA, in either the living or once having lived, to varying and inscrutable degrees, all things being individual and yet collective in their infinite expressions. Therefore, woman can know both Goddess and God, but by her very incarnate self it is the Lady that she represents; man can know both Goddess and God, but he is born as man, therefore it is God that he is here to express.

I haven't given you any human qualities associated with either Goddess or God, have I? I'm not going to because human qualities are human qualities and are irrelevant when discussing or considering that which is ineffable, inscrutable, immense, immanent, indivisible, and profound.

# A WITCH'S GODDESS

A witch's primary power (deity) is her/his Goddess. She is known by many names, derived from many cultures, and all are aspects of the One. The Moon in its waxing and waning, in its phases of full, new, and dark, is how witches dance with the birth, life, and death of their undertakings and their experiences. Through ritual and observance we align ourselves with our Goddess in Her ancient, but perennial, robes of maiden, mother, and crone. A priestess will "draw down the Moon," a process of invocation, within herself to awaken and empower that within each of us that is essentially *of* the Goddess.

She is also the Earth and is known by Her ancient names of Dana, Demeter, Isis, Inanna, Gaia, Brigid, Aphrodite, and Cerridwen, as well as the many others known by individuals and cultures alike. She is a warrior-goddess, known by such names as Ishtar, Brigantia, Artemis, and Nemesis. She is Goddess of the dark places, the Underworld, the unconscious, the Fates, and, especially, sorcery and Witchcraft. She is Persephone, Hecate, Isis, Tiamat, Morgan le-fey, Cerridwen, Diana, and Aradia.

She is Goddess of the stars and space and sea and, therefore, She is Binah, Astarte, Mari, Asherah, Arianrhod. She is Goddess of wisdom, learning, and the arts. She is Sophia, Shekinah, Binah, Isis, Vivienne. She is the path of the incarnate priestess and witch who is Her representative in our world, and She dwells in seed within all that is female. She is the sister, lover, mother, ally, and enemy to all that is male, a necessary interplay for the ways of life and death.

Her invocation within priestess and woman makes an inevitable difference to both self and society. The reverence, passion, and honor given freely to Her by Her priests assures witches of easy alliances irrespective of sexual distinction. There has been an historically trackable wave of imbalance since the ideology of one male, omnipotent God became a politically expedient and suppressive tactic, predominantly over the last 1,673 years, principally since the Council of Nicea in 325 C.E., when heresy became the "in" crime and the subsequent subjugation of women, culture, learning, freedom, wisdom, and honor were the expedient. The glory of conquest, greed, ownership, power for power's sake, bigotry, and aggression became the acceptable paradigm. A semblance of rebalancing has begun in the late twentieth century, but there is much to redress.

## FULL MOON

The ways of magic are aligned with the Full Moon. The archetypes of both Goddess and God resonate with a liberating consciousness, and the Ritual of Esbat (the rite of the Full Moon) releases the vision of balance into the astral and thence into the collective mind of our species.

## NEW MOON

The New Moon is intended to aid the growth of new endeavors—that which is begun at this time can be seen in its completion (this applies to short-term projects) by the time the Moon is full. It is the time of the maiden, the virgin (which means owned by no man), and much spellcasting is done by witches at this time of the lunar cycle. That which is planted at the time of the New Moon grows stronger and in accordance with its pattern more so than at other times.

# Dark Moon

The waning and subsequent Dark Moon are, interestingly, very active times for practical magic. (This applies to many, many witches with whom I have spoken in the Southern Hemisphere. It is, or so I have been told, different in the Northern Hemisphere. I would like to learn why this is so.) The Dark Moon is also a time for introspection, study, and assessment of one's own progress.

# The Four Fire Festivals
# (Known as the Greater Sabbats)

The Fire Festivals interweave themselves with the lesser Sabbats of solstice and equinox, but whereas the solstices and equinoxes mark the transitions of the Sun in its association with the Earth, the Fire Festivals mark the transitions of the *seasons* of Earth, the initiation of the transitions that are actualized and obvious at solstice and equinox.

Both Goddess and God are representative of all of the eight Sabbats of the Wheel, but, like day follows night, and as inherent in the day is the night (and vice versa), one face of this dual force will seem more manifest than the other in either the Fire Festivals or the Solar/Earth Sabbats.

The Wheel of the Fire Festivals progresses as follows: Samhain (also known, more recently and as a result of the Christianizing of this festival, as Halloween, or All Hallows); the Feast of Bride (also known as Imbolc); Beltaen (also known as Beltane); and Llughnassad (also known as Oimelc and, resulting from the Christianizing of this Sabbat, as Candlemas).

# ESSENTIAL SYMBOLISM OF THE FOUR FIRE FESTIVALS

**Samhain:** The Feast of the Dead. The celebration of the reign of the dark Goddess, Queen of the Underworld. The time when the veil-between-the-worlds is thinnest. Samhain initiates winter.

**The Feast of Bride:** The rise of the child Goddess, virgin queen, Goddess of all wild things. The time of the-waking-of-the-world. The Feast of Bride initiates spring.

**Beltaen:** The Great Rite of the Goddess. Sacred marriage to the Sun King through his rite of the hunt. The summoning of the power of the Great Stag; celebration of fecundity. Beltaen initiates summer.

**Llughnassad:** Festival of the Goddess of Magic. The time of enchantment's queen; the power of the initiator is celebrated here, and the passage of the sacrifice of God (initiation proper); rite of the high priestess, Goddess incarnate. Llughnassed celebrates the light-bringer and the harvest, and it initiates autumn.

# A WITCH'S GOD

The witch's God has been denied! In His many masks He has been debased, despised, and relegated to a power of evil by a subjugative regime that reviles passion and individuality. You see, our God's presence in earlier cultures was such a threat to the wiles of the church, simply *because* of His potency, that they had to formulate their devil (circa sixteenth century) in His likeness in an attempt to staunch His influence and deride His people. He is the Lord of the Dance, and His ways are wild and bountiful. He is Lord of the Hunt; King Stag; the Green Man, Lord of the Forests; King of the Land, and Lord of the Underworld; Warrior, Enchanter, and Wild Thing—not concepts of God that the missionaries of the church wished to see revered in the hearts of the people they sought to convert and conquer!

To different cultures, He was known as the bull, the stag, the lion, the bear, the eagle, and the ram. He is named Dionysis, Osiris, Dumuzi, Herne, Apollo, Cu Chulainn, Aengus Og, Yeheshuah, Baphomet, Cernunnos, Llugh, Lucifer, Zeus, Baal, Shamash, Shaitan, Odin, Thor, and Pan. He is Arthur, Merlin, Lancelot, Gwidion, Galahad, and most definitely, Robin Hood! Many of the planets are allotted one of His many names. Most of the days of the week are named for Him. He is known as the Lord of Life and the Lord of Death, is both the good guy and the bad guy, defender and destroyer.

What is life but all these things? Even in the Christian legends, Jesus is known as "first star of the evening." Lucifer is considered the Morning Star; but that's Venus! It's all one light! Venus is also the Goddess, whether as Stellar Maris or Mari Lucifer.

As Dion Fortune wrote, "All Gods are one God, all Goddesses are one Goddess and there is but one initiator." So, it is so.

He is consort, brother, son, ally, and enemy of women, and He is the archetype of all men. Sometimes I figure that's why so many seem so lost—it is powerful for the spirit to recognize one-self in the archetype of the divine. The images presented to humanity by monotheists can never be identified with the ever-sorrowful, lustless mother/virgin, the ever-meek, ever-so-perfect, sacrificial lamb, despite that, at the source, these two are Goddess and God![18]

## SOLSTICE AND EQUINOX
## (KNOWN AS THE FOUR LESSER SABBATS)

The Wheel of Solstice and Equinox is as follows: Winter Solstice (known as Yule); to Spring Equinox (known as Ostara); to Summer Solstice (known as Litha); thence to Autumn Equinox (known as Mabon). This is the Solar/Earth Wheel.

We ritually acknowledge the solstice and equinoctial processions to align ourselves with these cycles, both personally and environmentally. The mythological symbolism is very important, as it is the *image* of the cycle that is out there that allows each witch to personalize the sacred drama as it begins to unfold. The cycle is, therefore, also a process and a progression of the initiate, both as person and priesthood, that spirals you out to dance the season of the Earth. The way of a witch is irrevocably interwoven with these progressions, the point being that *all that is* runs through your veins, and to celebrate this is what your priesthood is about. It is also important to understand that our planet, supporting as she does the myriad and diverse life forms and patterns, *must* be empathized with to be understood. She is not just a patch of dirt to be exploited for her bounty.

Living the Wheel enables us to flow more freely with our individual destinies. It enables us to achieve by flowing with the pattern rather than with the dominant paradigm. The Solar/Earth progression awakens (after the sleep of darkness, marked by

Samhain) at the Winter Solstice (the first phase of the waxing year) and continues through spring, summer, and autumn. Interwoven with these Sabbats are the Fire Festivals.

## ESSENTIAL SYMBOLISM OF SOLSTICE AND EQUINOX

**Winter:** Rebirth of the Sun God. The boyhood and training of the once and future king.

**Spring:** Symbolic and actual mating of the Sun King with the daughter and priestess of the Moon. His initiation as both priest and king.

**Summer:** Sacrifice of the Sun King, leading to the harvest of his reign. Transformation.

**Autumn:** His descent into the realms of the Underworld. Power from the Dark Lord to the Virgin Queen of Initiation.

# THE EIGHT-FOLD WHEEL OF THE YEAR

| Sabbat | Southern Hemisphere | Northern Hemisphere |
| --- | --- | --- |
| Samhain | May 1 | October 31 |
| Winter Solstice | June 21 (approx.) | December 21 (approx.) |
| Feast of Bride | August 2 | February 2 |
| Spring Equinox | September 21 (approx.) | March 21 (approx.) |
| Beltaen | October 31 | May 1 |
| Summer Solstice | December 21 (approx.) | June 21 (approx.) |
| Llughnassad | February 2 | August 2 |
| Autumn Equinox | March 21 (approx.) | September 21 (approx.) |

Witches work ritual at each of these Sabbats, and at the correct phases of the Moon, throughout the Wheel of the Year.

## *The Pattern*

Within the following story, the symbolic interplay between myth, magic, and the revolution (the Wheel of the Year) are displayed. Please contemplate.

*Within time, as without, there exists a lineage as old as Time—the lineage is the Merlin and the lineage is the Morgan, the Force of the Wisest in the ways of Magic, both male and female, who are of the Great Sea, the Veil-Between-the-Worlds.*

*The Force of Merlin is summoned into the form of the Wisest of Men; the Force of Morgan is summoned into the Form of the Wisest of Women, and They know each other always.*

*Of the Four Fire Festivals, we all know. Of the four, the Wisest of Queens is the Queen who wears the Crown of Morgan-le-fey, Whose presence is felt at the Time of Samhain. She never quite dwells outside of the Mists, but Her Form is seen in the Priestess of the Moon, both upon the Island-Outside-of-Time and in the World-Within-Time.*

*Know the Legend! For if the Legend were to die, so would the Magic. Magic is the Gate-Between-the-Worlds, and* the Gate must be kept open.

*So, understand the above and listen, with mind and heart, to the legend . . .*

*In the Caves beneath the World there exists many things, like Dragons and Merlins and Sleeping Kings. To awaken the Latter*

*we must summon the Former—the Power of the Sacred Seed!
It blossoms within the Womb of an Ancient Queen Who does not
age, nor lose Her ability to bear fruit. Her representative in Time
is the Priestess of the Moon who is not known, nor acknowledged,
within the World of Men. She bears the Dragon through the
Darkness and to the Daughters of the Moon is born a Son: He-
Who-will-Be-King.*

*He is taught, by the Merlin, many things.*

*He is taught to See, to Walk, to Listen, to Remember, to Learn
for Himself. He is taught to Talk, to honor all things of the
Sacred, to Defend Himself; He is taught the power of Defend-
ing more than Himself. He is taught the Speech of Air, of Fire,
of Water, of Earth and he is taught to do with what He learns!
He learns of the Sacred Places. He is given to understand the
Instruments of Magic and how they are wielded. He learns
about Beauty. He learns about Pain. He is taught Compassion
and also Justice. He is taught to question and to seek the Truth
in all things.*

*He is given the Power to keep open the Gates-Between-the-Worlds
and to know which of Them is which!*

*Not much more than a boy is He . . . but He is ready.*

*He comes to the Island-Outside-of-Time, the Sacred Place that is
known to all who tread the Path of Magic, at the Time of Spring.
The Daughters of the Moon choose from amongst themselves. The
Force of Morgan is summoned and invoked within Her by all of
them, but especially by the Wisest of Women, Queen of the Lake.*

*The Boy must prove Himself to the Daughters of the Moon; the Rite of Manhood sees Him running with Stag, on the wildest of Wild Hunts, to seek the right to His Crown. The Lady Morgan awaits Him and sends Him Her strength. He takes the Crown!*

*The Lady Morgan anoints His body with perfumed oils and together They enter the Bower of Flowers that has been prepared for Them.*

*"As the Cup is as both woman and Goddess and Athame is both as man and as God so it is by Their Union that all is Bountiful!"*

*. . . with the Dawn They come, loving each other and the One-Who-is-Yet-to-Be. The Queen of the Lake hands Him Her Sword, most Sacred of the Sacred Regalia within the Caves of the Blessed Isle, as yet within its blood-red Scabbard, and says to Him: "One is nothing without the Other . . . Justice and Compassion is the Law of the Sword." . . . and He returns to within Time to defend the Places of the World and so to fulfill His purpose.*

*He grows Strong in Truth and His Power is known throughout the Land and the People sing His praises, "Oh, Beloved of the Lady!" and the Earth bears Fruit.*

*. . . but the Wheel spins and spins and His Fruitfulness is replaced with the Wisdom of the Age . . . and He knows His stay within Time has run its course—the Harvest begins! and His Body is scattered throughout the Fields; He is corn and oats and wheat and barley and all the fruit and flesh and grain of the Time.*

*. . . and His remains are deep within the Earth and the Land lies waiting the Child-of-Promise . . . and it all begins again*

*. . . and again*

*. . . and again*

—Ly de Angeles

# THE ELEMENTS (PART 2)
# SIGNIFICANCE IN RITUAL AND
# IN THE WAY OF THE SACRED

The four elements are both a protective and a balancing factor in Witchcraft. You learned in Part One of their importance in self-training through understanding and the work of the *Book of Elements*. Here you will work with them in a different way.

## Exercise 1

Please take note of the following associations so that you are aware of their corresponding symbols and entities. You will need to know this prior to the practical rituals that follow.

# Earth

**Direction:** South in the Southern Hemisphere, North in the Northern Hemisphere

**Time of Day:** Midnight

**Time of Year:** Winter

**Ritual Tools:** Pentacle and salt

**Tarot Association:** Pentacles

**Signs of the Zodiac:** Taurus, Virgo, Capricorn

**Color:** Black

**Archangelic Principle:** Uriel

**Elemental King:** Ghobb

**Elementals:** Gnomes

**Chayoth ha-Qadesh:** the Winged Bull

**Hermetic Axiom:** "To Know"

**Of the Holy Regalia:** The Shield

# Air

**Direction:** East

**Time of Day:** Dawn

**Time of Year:** Spring

**Ritual Tools:** Athame, sword, and incense

**Tarot Association:** Swords

**Signs of the Zodiac:** Libra, Aquarius, Gemini

**Color:** Pale yellow and pale blue

**Archangelic Principle:** Raphael

**Elemental King:** Paralda

**Elementals:** Sylphs

**Chayoth ha-Qadesh:** the Angel, or Androgyn—Adam Kadmon

**Hermetic Axiom:** "To will"

**Of the Holy Regalia:** Excalibur

# Fire

**Direction:** North in the Southern Hemisphere, South in the Northern Hemisphere

**Time of Day:** Midday

**Time of Year:** Summer

**Ritual Tools:** Wand, staff, and altar candle

**Tarot Association:** Wands

**Signs of the Zodiac:** Aries, Leo, Sagittarius

**Color:** Red

**Archangelic Principle:** Michael

**Elemental king:** Djinn

**Elementals:** Salamanders

**Chayoth ha-Qadesh:** the Winged Lion

**Hermetic Axiom:** "To Dare"

**Of the Holy Regalia:** the Spear

# Water

**Direction:** West

**Time of Day:** Sunset

**Time of Year:** Autumn

**Ritual Tools:** Chalice (also called the cup), the cauldron, and consecrated Water

**Tarot Association:** Cups

**Signs of the Zodiac:** Cancer, Scorpio, Pisces

**Color:** Purple/blue

**Archangelic Principle:** Gabriel (pronounced Gavriel)

**Elemental King:** Nixsa

**Elementals:** Undines

**Chayoth ha-Qadesh:** the Eagle

**Hermetic Axiom:** "To Keep Silence"

**Of the Holy Regalia:** the Grail

# A WITCH'S MOST-VALUED POSSESSIONS (THE INSTRUMENTS, TOOLS, AND WEAPONS OF THE ART)

I will describe what you will require and the order of their acquisition. You will be capable of working ritually with the minimum of requirements, but overall, there are many things I am not including that you might acquire only as is needed.

## Athame—Black-Handled Dagger

Pronounced ath-em-ay, this weapon is obtained *as soon as possible* by the trainee witch. It is a dagger with a double-edged blade. It is your weapon of intent. The hilt of the dagger is to be black. You can paint it, or cover it in leather or velvet. It can be as decorous or as simple as you desire. Once you have your athame, you will use it always (it's meant to be the first and only one you'll have while you are alive, like your body). Contrary to some opinions, once it is consecrated to you, it can *never* be deconsecrated; just like you, once you take initiation, you can *never* be deinitiated. It's rubbish to think that could happen. So be aware!

The athame is used to cast a ritual circle, to invoke, summon, consecrate, bind, banish, awaken, and charge all that is of the power! The blade is always magnetized before use—that enlivens it. You must be sure that you put energy into the preparation of your dagger; don't just pick one up at a shop and leave it as it is: you must art it.

The athame is *never* used to draw blood. It is *never* used by anyone else. When not in use, it is to be secreted away (as all your ritual things must be). It is associated with Air △. The consecration of your athame is in Part Two of Section Two.

## The Cup—Chalice

The cup is traditionally a silver, or silver-like, with a goblet shape. It is a Moon cup, silver being the metal of the Moon, although I have seen them made from clay, wood, crystal, and horn. The cup is the symbol of our Goddess in a ritual, and, as such, it is as important to have it present in your circle as it is to have your athame. When it is filled, for whatever purpose, it becomes the vessel of a sacred fluid, be it wine or water, that fills the initiate with the properties of its nature. It is traditional, always, to drink from the cup-of-plenty at any ritual. The cup is associated with Water ▽.

## The Boline—White-Handled Dagger

This is a practical dagger that can be used in your ritual circle and in your day-to-day use—*but not by anyone else!* The blade can be double-edged or single-edged, sickle or curved, it matters not. It is consecrated to your use by your athame (as is everything else you will use in a ritual way). It is used for cutting herbs for specific use, preparing food, carving the wand and staff, dressing candles, when hunting, and, if the need should arise, self-defense. When not in use it, too, is to be kept away from others' use.

## The Pentacle

The pentacle is a disc traditionally made of copper, but wood is okay if copper is unobtainable. It is cut to about fourteen centimeters in diameter (approximately a hand-span) and is inscribed with the seal of the pentagram, as well as any other pertinent sigils that you deem appropriate. It is a tool for summoning and controlling certain powers, and for banishing.

After having inscribed it as above, prepare your pentacle for ritual use by burying it in the earth in the path of the passing Moon at the time of the New Moon. Leave it there until the Full

Moon, when you will dig it up and consecrate it with the Ritual of Esbat. If it is copper, it will have turned green within that time—that's okay, the pentacle is allocated to Venus, and is associated with Earth $\triangledown$.

## The Wand

The wand is *always* handcrafted. It may be simple or carved, inscribed, or painted with the sigils of magic. There are two types of wands—one that will be of permanent use as your ritual wand, and others that will be created for specific purposes, when needed, and then buried after use. The wand is used to symbolize the active power of Fire in any ritual; as such it is an instrument of summoning.

The length of your wand will be from (approximately) the tip of your middle finger to the inside of your elbow. It is cut and carved from one of the traditionally sacred woods: foremost is willow, a wood most sacred for the symbolism of its bending and flowing; then there is hazel, oak, rowan, hawthorn, blackthorn, birch, beech, applewood, and elm. The wood is not to be taken from a productive tree. Either wait until winter dormancy or until the branch is dead. The wand is associated with Fire $\triangle$.

## Censer

You will need a censer (also called a thurible, brazier, or incense burner) and incense. You will be burning incense throughout most of your rituals, and making your own is always preferable to joss sticks. Some well-known occult supply outlets have people make up specific incenses for sale. Most of these are usually beautiful and I recommend them if you cannot make your own.

The censer can be of any material that will withstand heat, but whatever it is, it should be aesthetically acceptable for a sacred space. Place sand or soil in the bottom of your container and have some wire mesh to support the charcoal block on which the mixture of incense is to burn. You will need air under the block for effective burning.

## Incense

Incense is made by mixing equal amounts of sandalwood powder and either frankincense, myrrh (which will need to be ground lightly with mortar and pestle), benzoin gum, or storax (which burns really fast), to which you will add several drops of whichever oil is pertinent to your working. The mixture should be slightly moist but not wet. Self-igniting charcoal blocks can be acquired from Catholic supply shops in Australia (probably the same in the Northern Hemisphere), or in foils from many health food outlets (although these cost more than buying in bulk from the Catholic shop).

It is preferable to make incense in preparation for each working. A suitable vessel to hold it and a small pair of tongs for serving it to the censer will also be required. Incense is associated with Air △.

## Five Candlesticks

One particular candlestick for your altar flame (without the light from which no ritual is activated) and four others for each of the gates of Earth, Air, Fire, and Water.

## Robe

Robing is a sometime thing. Witches often work skyclad (naked) or part thereof, but robing is often not only practical but necessary. The robe is to be of a natural fiber, as this does not impede body magnetism like synthetics do. It is also to be, at least in part, handstitched. The robe is most often a cloak with a hood, which is particularly beneficial for inner plane voyaging or deep trance work. Your robe is to be whatever you consider beautiful, but remember that a lot of flowing and draping fabric can be dangerous when working around open flame, therefore it should also be practical.

## Other Tools

You will also need a container for your salt, rock salt for use in consecrations, a container for the water you will use for consecration, and cords for both marking the perimeter of a circle, when desired, and for certain kinds of Witchcrafting. You will need an amulet or talisman, which can also represent the robe and will give others of the Way the possibility of recognizing you in a public place. You will need a staff (can be with a tang) for certain ritual purposes, preferably made of a native hardwood and decorated to your desire. You will need oil, usually olive oil with a few drops of your preferred essential oil or oil blend, and a vial in which to store it. There are three books you will need. They are covered in the next section.

# Keeping Records—The Book of Shadows and Various Grimoires

## A Book of Shadows

This book could just as easily be called *A Book of Secrets* because it is a book that is yours only, forever, and not for public exhibition; a secret is no longer a secret when it is no longer a secret! My *Book of Shadows* is one of my precious possessions. The rituals in its pages are not only my secrets, but those of my coven and of the coven before me and of the covens before them. The rituals are specific to our line. That's not to say they are not known to others, they may very well be, but I have not shown them, and neither have the witches of my coven nor the witches of the covens before me. Each time one of the rituals in its handwritten, leather-bound pages is worked by either me or my coven, it is worked with all of the awe that accompanies a secret. A secret is kept, like an oath, so that the understanding of what it represents is never profaned. Inherent in the word "secret" is the term "special." Each witch that I initiate will faultlessly copy, into his or her own *Book of Shadows*, the legacy of sacred days that is specific to our inheritance.

That may, at first, seem to be a problem to you if you are using this book (and any other associated with the subject) to assist with your self-training, but it is not so. Most of the creditable works published in recent years present you with variations of their own *Books of Shadows* (not necessarily its specific content), thereby retaining their oaths that may very well pertain to keeping the book secret while giving you adequate guidelines for creating your own.

*What is integral is that you create your own* and choose to write up the rites of Sabbat and Esbat according to your cognizance of the material you research. A *Book of Shadows*, in addition to being a witch's book of secrets, is a work of art. I have not seen a fully created *Book of Shadows* that was not meant to be a legacy to the ancient future, that was created to be other than an ancient artifact, of incredible durability and beauty, that could be discovered by some ancestor two thousand years hence, and revered for its presence alone.

## Grimoires

All of a witch's records of important information and knowledge are, again, handwritten into volumes called *grimoires*. As such, although this is a published and typed work, it is (and has been) the result of almost thirty years of practical, working grimoires aimed at teaching future initiates the Ways of a witch.

These volumes are created with the same respect as one's *Book of Shadows* in that they are beautifully covered in leather of the highest quality and stored away from profane eyes. Because your grimoire will be filled with the notes, sentiments, recipes, techniques, and spells that are specific to you, it should be as neat or as messy or as extravagant or as detailed as any artist's or professor's would be (which is, of course, exactly what a witch tends to be, no matter how eccentric).

If I had not kept records over the years, I would not be constantly surprised by what I forgot that I know! You never knows when you will need to repeat a certain kind of spell in the future, and when you have worked a spell that *works*, it is best to remember the formula.

There is a power to hand writing and hand copying certain texts, as the exercise alone deepens the absorption of the material, as does the memorization of all, or most, of your *Book of Shadows*. Working ritual is best done when the ritual is a part of your second nature. There is no stumbling and there are no mistakes when the outline of a working (which is what the written ritual *is*) is so comfortable that it allows for more than itself.

## Dream Diaries

I will cover dreams, specifically, in Part Three. Your Dream Diary will do two things:

1.  It will keep a record of your dreams (pertinent or not, at the time).

2.  It will teach you over time to differentiate your dreams and to interpret them according to their type, perhaps assisting others, through your understanding, to interpret their own.

# THE HERMETIC QUATERNARY

## To Know

It is important that you accumulate sufficient knowledge of a diverse nature, in addition to the subjects that interest you, concerning the inheritance of your art. There is power in knowledge for its own sake (although not for the sake of accumulation only). All manner of related subjects can assist you in your work—things of an anthropological, religious, mythological, philosophic, scientific, artistic, historic, and psychological nature; the opinions of recognized and intelligent occultists; material pertinent to your quest (astrology, numerology, Tarot, hermetics, mysticism, Qabbalah, magic, legend, and the various traditions of Witchcraft). It is also advisable to acquire and perpetuate a physical discipline (the axiom "to know" relates to the element of Earth) to assist the physical form that you host (your body) in enjoying life's bounty to the maximum.

With all the information that you acquire, it is important that you take time to utilize the quality of discernment to enable you to ascertain the difference between what is hearsay on the part of the authors or experts concerned, and what rings true. All things are to be analyzed, which will lead you to a balanced and enriching viewpoint.

No information is wasted, and it's necessary to know enough to trust your own findings from deep within the occult places of yourself when they awaken. Ignorance is *never* bliss, and all material that you view can only extend, through reflection, your ability to live your Craft.

> **"To know" is the foundation of the triangle;**
> **being also the element of Earth;**
> **the pentacle and the shield.**

## To Will

In its lesser forms, the will (consider intent) of an adequately trained witch should be capable of directing his or her life, in accordance with both pattern and balance, to deep satisfaction, and, likewise, for great personal benefit as well as for the benefit of the evolving whole.

In its most intense form, the will is capable, circumstantially, of directing the course of events beyond the need of the individual, such as in cases of threat (either personally or collectively, which includes all biodiversity). In all cases, the energy raised is for *defense and resolution* rather than attack.

No magical implement of a material nature can be charged without the power of the focused and disciplined will (which will differ in each witch in accordance with his or her nature). No circle can be cast, neither can it defend; one cannot banish unwanted influences, nor maintain, let alone raise, power; no force can be invoked or evoked, and magic remains an intellectual concept or a triviality rather than an actuality without the power of the focused and disciplined will.

**"To will" is the right wall of the triangle;**
**being also the element of Air;**
**the athame and the sword (Excalibur).**

## To Dare

I am writing this on the hypothesis that you have done the training set out for you thus far (if you haven't, this won't do you any good at all!). You are, as a result, in a position to experiment with what you have learned. Refer to the technique of visualization and look to the sections whereby you created an event of an outside nature.

In considering that work, we dealt with what could be termed a working of the mundane kind. Now you are to focus your skills on the work of a magical nature and seek to deepen by way of interacting with the powers that are beneficent and malleable (please read the rest of the book before continuing with this exercise). Take care, in the initial stages, to interfere in no area that does not personally concern you. Where all acts of spellcrafting are concerned, do not exceed your own ability to handle the outcome (due to any unresolved sense of self-aggrandizement). To do so would get you into an awful mess and would waste power.

Say *nothing* to anyone of your experiment; to do so would doom it to failure.

To be clear in your communications, your actions, and your desires is the Way of bravery. There is no room in the Craft for whiners, wimps, hypocrisy, cowardice, pomposity, or any other of the acceptable masks of the inept. It takes courage to be unfettered. It also takes a degree of daring.

**"To Dare" is the left wall of the triangle;**
**being also the element of Fire;**
**the wand and the spear.**

## To Keep Silence

In all things this is a very important function (it is also a most underrated power). Unless you have the utmost faith in the integrity of the person with whom you desire to discuss the Way of witch, you will say nothing. Experience has taught that unless "your cup is full and overflowing," you will deplete what you want to store by tossing it around (and, after all, what is your motive?). Be aware that ignorance and bigotry toward Witchcraft is still rife in most lands where the dominant paradigm is "with us or against us" religions. They'd be okay if they didn't interfere in the ways of others, but they do!

The techniques of spellcrafting that work for you may not work for everyone, so there is no reason to dilute the power by discussing what you are doing with anyone who is not working on a project with you. Record all your successes in your personal grimoire of spells and incantations for future use.

*Remember—never boast, never threaten!*

Be guarded when working as a solitary witch regarding others you meet with whom you might choose to work. It is exciting when two or more witches practice together, but, as I said earlier in this work, some wear the trappings for an identity. It's always best to know someone for a time and to test the water. Therefore, speak not of what you know until you *become* that of which you speak, for a witch is what you *are* rather than something you *do*.

Silence is a profound teacher and a hard taskmaster. Learn her art when it is offered; there is much to hear within her temple!

"To Keep Silence" is the circle
that surrounds the other three tenets;
the element of Water;
the chalice and the grail.

# Section Two

# RITUAL PROPER

## REIVING

Reiving is clearing, cleaning, and preparing your place of work. The place where you are to cast your circle must be clear of all unnecessary bits and pieces (distractions!); the less you have around you, the less there is to consider. This is difficult only if you live with others who are not of a kind or if you don't have a room that you can set aside for use as a temple.

You will, however, find a way to have a clear space, be it indoor or outside, and to ascertain your privacy. You will sweep, dust, and wash any and all things *within the proximity of your circle* (anything else is not our concern here). You will do it in a state of contemplation and focus, intent on excellence, as though you were creating a most special gift for the person you love most in your life—that's reiving.

You will prepare the things that you will have with you for the ritual (make the incense, trim the wicks of the candles, have a bottle of good red wine or fruit juice, such as apple or grape, ready for the rite) being certain to omit nothing—that's reiving.

When the time is approaching, you will bathe or shower, still in the space of contemplation (you won't want to be drawn into conversation that is irrelevant to the magic), with the intention of neutralizing any energies that are not your own (it's got nothing to do with soap) and being clear of all things that could be extraneous to the working—that's reiving.

The final step of reiving is to ascertain that the doors are locked and the phone is off the hook, ensuring that you are undisturbed for as long as you desire.

# RITUAL
## PHASE ONE: TO CAST A RITUAL CIRCLE

The Prologue of *The Way of the Goddess* is the process of reiving and the preparation leading to the casting of a circle for the purpose of ritual, in story form. The technique described there is that of a witch who has, however, been about the business of Witchcraft for a very long time. The technique of casting a circle that you will work, according to this text, is that of a witch who has not, as yet, consecrated the necessary implements of the Craft. Please consider:

1.  What is called, in Witchcraft, a circle, is technically not a circle at all. You will cast your circle in a circular fashion, but the circle is actually a spherical force field, and you are *within* its web. When a circle is cast, it is cast along its equator (with the extended will directed out from the point of your athame, directing the magnetized field to surround yourself), and an interwoven network, or grid-pattern, of fine, luminous blue filaments expands outward to link above and below the immediate area at the polar points of zenith and nadir.

2.  Water is used in a sprinkling fashion prior to casting the circle to wet down any static associated with the field, just like wetting down one's body in the reiving process. The water that is used for this purpose is consecrated (made sacred through the focus and intent of the practitioner) prior to its use, and salt (similarly consecrated) is added for its conductive quality.

3.  Once the circle is cast, it is maintained throughout the rite by your awareness of it at the peripheral of your mind's eye.

## The Gates of the Elements

4. Gateways are then summoned into existence by using the seal of the invoking pentagram at the four compass points of south, east, north, and west. Guardians, of an elemental nature, are summoned for the duration of the ritual. The purpose of this is dual: (1) to allow the flow of your working to reach the substratum of the powers of life through their participation in the intent of the ritual, and (2) once summoned, they will serve as both sentinels and protectors of the sacred space that you have created.

Please note: in the preceding paragraph, I specifically positioned the compass points in a counterclockwise circular pattern—this is *sunwise* in the Southern Hemisphere. Here, the Sun and Moon rise to the east and proceed in a seemingly northern direction to reach their zenith due north; then set to the west. In the Northern Hemisphere, the Sun is at zenith due south, which is why your Fire element is opposite ours. So, in the northern lands, your circle is also cast sunwise (called deosil, or "with the sun"), but it is clockwise, whereas in the Southern Hemisphere when our circle is cast sunwise, still called deosil, it is counterclockwise.

## The Seals of Opening and Closing the Elemental Gates

These seals are pentagrams. They are inscribed into space at the gateway of their element, initially by your hand, and later by your athame. A pentagram is one continuous line, a symbol of power, so practice the invoking pentagrams until they are familiar. Pentagrams summon and protect, bind and banish, depending on how they are used. They are also one of the main symbols of a witch's amulet.

**To Invoke:** Begin the sigil at "I" and follow the arrow to invoke the seal that opens the elemental gate.

**To Banish:** Begin the sigil at "B" and follow the arrow to banish the seal that closes the elemental gate.

Earth
South: Southern Hemisphere
North: Northern Hemisphere

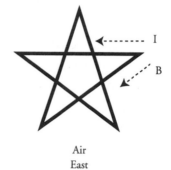

Air
East

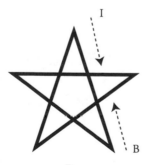

Fire
North: Southern Hemisphere
South: Northern Hemisphere

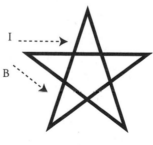

Water
West

5. Within your sacred space you will have an altar. It is placed at the midnight point of your circle. The midnight point is the place of all things possible, whereas dawn, midday, and sunset are obvious phases of life (i.e., the birth, growth, and fulfillment of any living thing) The midnight phase of life is the unseen or the unknown, the hidden phase of life, and is considered as an outside-of-time phase; hence "all things possible."

6. On your altar will be whatever you require for the specific rite.

Please note that it is not always necessary to summon the elemental guardians to your circle. Their alliance is not required when you are spellcrafting *unless* your spellcrafting has far-reaching ramifications or is dangerous; it is not necessary to summon them to a house-blessing or when casting a circle for certain practical purposes like consecrating new items for your temple or when speaking of practical magical intentions to another witch. You are advised, however, to cast a circle for such specific discussions.

## Exercise

1. Choose a night.

2. Reread the section titled A Witch's Most-Valued Possessions and ascertain what the bare necessities will be for a simple practical ritual exercise. This is the intent of this ritual. Allow me to advise: candles (five—one for your altar and one for each of the four gateways); water and salt in their individual containers; incense (at this stage, whatever you can procure); a white cord long enough to encompass the entirety of your sacred space. If, by now, you have gathered the things mentioned in the above section that are a witch's necessities,

(dagger for transformation to athame; goblet for transformation to cup/chalice; disc for the pentacle; branch for a wand, censer, etc.), then by all means, have them on your altar for this first exercise (just don't use them yet!).

3.  Reive the place where you will be working and set your things up (i.e., altar in its correct place; altar candle upon it; incense, water, and salt there, too; one well-secured candle on the floor at each of the compass points; matches to light the candles, and incense.)

4.  Bathe with the intent of purification (reive your body to cleanse it of the static built up through interaction with the day).

5.  Secure your privacy.

6.  Lay the cord around the perimeter of your temple, making sure that the two ends overlap. Light the candles, *beginning* with the altar candle and walking *deosil*, from south (north in the Northern Hemisphere) through east, north (south), west, and back to south, lighting the candles as you go.

    *At no time, during the rite, do you move in any direction other than deosil. This keeps the power flowing in accordance with the pattern—any and all movements being akin to dancing the circle's intent!*

7.  Seat yourself before the altar and prepare yourself as a vessel, as you were taught in Part One, Section One.

8.  When you are centered, take the container of water in one hand and describe the seal of the invoking pentagram of Earth over it. Using your visualization technique, you will see the pentagram in vivid electric-blue light. Then infuse the water with it. Replace the container of now-charged water

and do the same with the salt. Then mix the salt into the water. *This is now consecrated water!* (You can bottle this consecrated water and keep it in your secret place for use at other times. It is not necessary to create consecrated water each time you craft; however, it is advisable to add what little is left in this bottle when you create the next batch; it keeps the flow continuous (the same applies to your consecrated oil).

9. Walk the boundary of the circle, from south to south (north to north in the North Hemisphere), being conscious of the understanding and the vision of what this circle is. Walk slowly so you can control the process involved in the casting of the circle.

   Note: Many texts have been written using words to cast one's circle. I have definitely found that words get in the way here, but if they work for you, then use them.

10. Summon the guardian of the gate of Earth (south in the Southern Hemisphere; north in the Northern Hemisphere) by tracing the invoking pentagram of Earth with your hand at the appropriate compass point of your circle. Summon the guardian of Air with the relevant invoking pentagram at the eastern compass point of your circle. Do likewise for Fire at the northern point (southern point in the Northern Hemisphere) and for Water at the western point.

11. Now take the time to sit and contemplate your place of ritual and what you have achieved.

12. That area will not be the same once you have worked it.

13. When you have given yourself adequate time in this manner, go to the gate of Earth and silently honor the powers of that element before you describe the relevant banishing pentagram; likewise for the other elements.

14. Extinguish your altar candle and break the seal of the circle by opening the cord.

15. To ground and center yourself after ritual, you can do one of two things: (1) stand with your legs akimbo and breathe your energy into the floor or earth, or (2) eat.

## PHASE TWO: CONSECRATION AND EMPOWERING YOUR ATHAME

Once you have completed this section, you'll be ready, if you choose, to take the steps of self-initiation (should you be unable to locate a copacetic coven to take you through).

This time you will have a proper censer and specially prepared incense. You will also have prepared your pentacle and wand, and you will most certainly have procured your chalice. Ascertain that you have a magnet to charge the blade of your dagger.

Please read this ritual through several times and commit it to memory, if possible (have it handwritten, anyway, and with you in your circle).

### Requirements

1. The above.

2. Your dagger (already wiped well down both sides of the blade with the magnet).

3. Wine in the chalice, consecrated water, your vial of oil, and five candles and their holders.

Note: your oil will not be acceptable for use until it is infused with a minute quantity of your own essence (saliva, a blooddrop, tears, semen, or vaginal secretions). *No one is permitted to use your personal oil for any reason thereafter.* Do not allow the vial to completely dry up at any time; top it up before that happens.

Do not eat a heavy meal for quite a while before this rite.

Reive and prepare as you did in the last exercise (but this is a rite of power and not considered an exercise), and have your athame, chalice, pentacle, and wand on the altar along with the censer and incense, the vial of prepared oil, and the altar flame.

# THE RITE

Light the candles and the incense, and seat yourself before your altar to center yourself. When you are focused, cast your circle as you have been taught. Then go to the gate of Earth, raise your arms, and summon the powers . . .

> **Come ye, of the Southern Winds,**
> **Place of storms and deepest Night,**
> **Place of silence most profound,**
> **Guard this circle set outside of Time.**
> **Acknowledge the purpose of this Rite!**
> **Open for me the Gate of Earth!**

You will then describe the seal of the invoking pentagram of Earth. Note: in the Northern Hemisphere, you will call on the northern winds at the gate of Earth.

Walk deosil to the gate of Air, raise your arms, and summon the powers . . .

> **Come ye, of the East Winds,**
> **Place of first Sun and rise of Moon,**
> **Place of Inspiration,**
> **Guard this circle set outside of Time.**
> **Acknowledge the purpose of this Rite!**
> **Open for me the Gate of Air!**

Cast the seal of the invoking pentagram of Air. Walk deosil to the gate of Fire, raise your arms, and summon the powers . . .

**Come ye, of the Northern Winds,**
**Place of the highest Sun,**
**Place of Creation manifest,**
**Guard this circle set outside of Time.**
**Acknowledge the purpose of this Rite!**
**Open for me the Gate of Fire!**

Cast the invoking pentagram of Fire. These are the powers of the southern winds in the Northern Hemisphere.

Go deosil to the western gate, raise your arms, and summon . . .

**Come ye, of the West Winds,**
**Place of the setting Sun,**
**Home of the Island Remembered,**
**Place of Wisdom;**
**Guard this circle set outside of Time.**
**Acknowledge the purpose of this Rite!**
**Open for me the Gate of Water!**

Describe the invoking pentagram of Water.

You are then to take the consecrated water and sprinkle it, deosil, around the perimeter of the circle.

Return to your altar.

Take up your dagger and wipe it all over with consecrated water; hold it tightly to your body; fully will your power into it! You will then kiss your athame on both sides of the blade and the hilt.

## To Bring the Athame to Life

To cause your athame to awaken to the powers of Earth, you will place the athame on the pentacle, raise it up, and say, slowly:

> By the Dance
> And in the Darkness
> By the Door and by the Drum
> By Enchantment
> The Eye of Midnight,
> The Inner Shield
> I bid thee come!

Wait until you sense the field, then say:

> **The Element of Earth infuse my Blade!**

To cause it to awaken to the powers of Air, refuel the censer, hold your athame in the smoke, and slowly say:

> By the Bridge that spans the River;
> By the Book—the Shadow Tome;
> By the Breath, the Sword of Wisdom,
> By Tuatha'n Bow
> I bid thee come!

Wait until you sense them, and then say:

> **Element of Air infuse my Blade!**

To cause your athame to awaken to the powers of Fire, you will hold it with the blade passing in and out of the flame of the altar candle and slowly say:

By the Seed beneath the Snow;
By the Finger of the Flame;
By the Forge, the power of Shaping;
By Stellar Fire
I bid thee come!

Wait until you sense them, then say:

**The Element of Fire infuse my Blade!**

To awaken your athame to the powers of Water, place the tip of your athame into the consecrated Water and slowly say:

**By the Queen of Ancient Magic!**
**By the Rainbow in the Storm!**
**By the Lake, the Isle Remembered!**
**By Sea of Space**
**I bid thee come!**

Wait until you feel them infuse your dagger, and say, lastly:

**The Element of Water infuse my Blade!**

For the consecration to be complete, you are to do two more things: (1) With much passion and focus, place the tip of your athame into the cup of wine and charge it with the concept of conjunctio (symbolic sacred sexual union). Place your athame in your lap while you drink from the cup. (2) Gently oil the blade with your specially prepared oil.

Take your athame, go deosil around your circle honoring each element in their turn, and using your will, extended through the blade, describe each banishing pentagram. Extinguish the candles.

Open the circle by drawing the energy of the force field into the blade of your athame. Then place the point into the ground to discharge it into the earth.

Put all your ritual things away before you do anything—then have something to eat to ground yourself.

Well done!

# Phase Three: The Process of Self-Initiation

We come so far and often know that we can go no further without a milestone, without crossing some unseen, but potent line. There's something about taking initiation that is akin to the first time we had sex—it marks the passage of girl to woman or boy to man more so than any other rite of passage.

The difference between initiation and one's first sexual encounter is that one's first sexual encounter is not always as clear-cut a matter of choice. They both, however, access certain powers of creativity that would remain dormant otherwise.

If you have challenged the sincerity of your desire, and know that the Way of witch is the most certain thing in your life; if witch is what you feel, then witch is what you are—so you cross the line.

This rite affirms you as what is called a solitary, but it does not preclude you from joining a coven (*as* a duly initiated witch), should you choose, and should you find one synchronistic to your individuality. They will either honor your self-initiation or seek to have you go through again at their hands. It will be your choice, as well as theirs, but what you do here is as true and effective an initiation as any other you might take. This is your first!

Step one is to take a full lunar month to seek your name. A witch's initiation name is their true name—and it is both secret and sacred. It contains all the essences of your power and is *never* spoken of unless it is to another initiate in whom you have absolute trust. You may receive your name during periods of ritual or visualization, from the significance of an association with myth or legend, or inspirationally. It will always be appropriate to your chosen path and symbolic of your aspirations.

## THE RITUAL

It is required that you enter into a personal initiation as seriously as if you were being initiated at the discretion of a witch of High Priesthood. Therefore, you will be required to fast from sunset of the day before until the dark of the night you have chosen, and to speak as little as possible (preferably not at all). Contemplation is part of the preparation. You are to be between-the-worlds for this time.

You are to learn the ritual by rote. You can tape the journey and play it at the appropriate time (your tape player is to be battery-operated as you won't have an electrical cable crossing the border of your circle), but have it written in your *Book of Shadows*, and have this book in your circle with you (as well as a pen).

### Requirements

1.  A silver pentagram necklace. This is your gift of initiation to yourself and also the symbol of your own commitment (there are many amulets and talismans that are worn by witches the world over that are specific to their own lineage, but the pentagram is an acknowledged symbol by all occultists).

2.  A bottle of very good red wine (or fruit juice if you desire something nonalcoholic).

3. Four candles (colors of your choice) for the elemental gateways, one black and one white candle (representing the understanding of duality) for the altar, and one white candle for your altar candle.

4. Prepare a *specific* oil for this night, sufficient to cover your whole body, but have your vial of magical oil on the altar. You will use it tonight for the second time.

5. Have all ritual equipment and tools within the circle with you (don't forget matches or a lighter), as well as your *Book of Shadows*, a pen, and the tape player and tape of the journey.

6. The ritual is to be worked within the boundary of the white cord.

Between sunset and full dark of the day of your initiation, you will reive and set up your sacred space in preparation. Bathe with intent. Have all necessary things on the altar (including the silver pentagram necklace and the bowl of specially prepared oil) within the boundary of your circle.

Make the incense of your choice and pour the wine into the cup.

*Be certain that you will not be disturbed.*

Cast the circle as you have learned. Move deosil at all times.

Light only the candle in the west (do not invoke any of the guardians at this time).

Seat yourself before your altar and prepare yourself as you have learned. When you are ready, make the sign of the invoking pentagram of Earth with your athame over the container of specially prepared oil, then rub your entire body with it saying:

**I, (name), am properly prepared
to take the rite of initiation.
I have no fear. I am committed to this.
I have two perfect words, Love and Trust,
and with all things I will uphold my oath rightly.**

Start the tape of the journey. Be seated on the ground with your knees drawn up, your arms around them, and your head resting on your arms for the entire journey.

Note: I use "we" and "I" and "the rider" in particularly interwoven fashion throughout the journey to indicate both you and you-within-the-vision. Don't let it disturb you. Once you've read the vision through, you'll understand.

## The Journey Between the Worlds

*I see before me the Tunnel of Time. I project myself toward this place and am drawn down and down, back and back, way, way back to before the dawn of Christendom in a land of emerald green and ageless beauty.*

*I am flying low over rolling hills and moorlands, circling freely over forests and small hamlets of country folk, over manor and mere heading toward an inevitable destiny.*

*I slow and close the distance between my world and this. The timelessness of a winter's night is silent; not even the sounds of the hawk or the owl can be heard through the thickening pall. I descend.*

*Now I hear muffled sounds from the marshland below me. I come to ground level where the mist is not so thick, but moving, steadily shapeshifting as it swirls around the mire.*

*There! Just ahead, on horseback, holding high a lantern to pick a path through this desolate place, is the horse and rider that I have been seeking.*

*I swoop slowly and land, as a mist, upon the horse's rump.*

*We think of naught; we must not lose our thoughts upon any other theme than that of following the almost imperceptible path through this empty place.*

*No life here. The lights of a thousand lost souls glint through the mist to remind us of our peril, but we hesitate not and heed not their warnings. My destiny burns within my soul and would destroy me were it not fulfilled.*

*I can see myself clearly by the light of the lantern; outlined with the ravages of many a sleepless night, I am gaunt. My jaw twitches with my effort, and my eyes are haunted by the dream. I am physically strong, cat-like. I clench the lantern, vice-like, in my hand. My clothing is simple: thonging criss-crossing the furs about my calves and woolen leggings as thick as mail about my thighs. My jerkin is the skin of a wolf snared in some past day and my cloak is russet and of heavy woven wool that hangs limply along the sides of my mount. I wear a hood of leather, but my hair lays in tangled rivulets down my back.*

*The length, thus far, of my journey lays heavily upon me, and my shoulders are bent forward with fatigue; but we may not stop until we are past this dreadful place.*

*Hour upon hour we move, well into the midnight, until at last the horse raises her head and snorts as she stumbles onto the grassland. We travel slowly still until the rider is certain of our bearings, then we roar with triumph and we are off, running like the wind, as the plain thunders beneath us!*

*We slow as dawn creeps above the horizon in a washed-out blur, and horse and rider, sweating at their efforts, breathe deeply at the sight. We come at length to a copse of trees into which we walk. We dismount and lead our beloved mare into the depths. There, a stream, cool and deep, at which we drink before we lead the horse to graze beneath the oaks and peer around, cautiously, to guess that none come here often; that we might have peace for a few hours during which we will rest.*

*I know not why, but know it I do, that the rider wishes to be seen by no one, so we ride by night and hide by day so that none may know that we are abroad.*

*We unsaddle the mare, crooning to her as we do so, and rub her down with the blanket from beneath the saddle. A smile crosses the rider's face, and a look that stirs my soul with its intensity and passion. Our task done, we proceed to prepare a small fire over which we roast potatoes and a strip of dried meat. We draw a leather flask from our pouch from which we quaff deeply, the contents sweet and fiery. Having eaten of our simple meal, we stamp the fire and curl within the cloak to sleep away the daylight hours.*

*And so I watch . . .*

*. . . at one point I rise above the trees and seek to ascertain our safety, for although the rider is furtive and afeared of notice, I ache for the quest, knowing it is also my own, and my compassion reaches out to the strength within our sleeping form who would do no harm without good cause. I know not how I would rouse us should danger approach, but there is no farm or village within distance, so I fear not for us.*

*I return to find us turning about restlessly in our sleep, the dream causing much mumbling and sighing; and so it is for a few hours more until I am woken by my own shouts. Sweat beads upon my face, and I stand and remove my hood and cloak, and walk to the stream to wash myself, and so lose the dreaming. I again light the fire and draw from my pouch a large cup that I fill from the stream. I brew a draught of strong herbs to help me to wakefulness for the long night ahead.*

*My journey will be done, thus far, on this night—at least where riding is concerned. The journey of the rest of my life is just beginning, the end of which is assured in my mind. There is no turning back from what I so earnestly seek but what I so earnestly dread, for it is unclear to me what ventures will befall me between the present moment and some eventual death.*

*I stamp the fire and cover its remains with dirt and brambles so that none may know that any had passed this way. I call to my horse and she comes from her grazing by the stream. I saddle her and attach my pouch to my belt. I don hood and cloak, and mount. We move slowly through the trees in the direction of the setting sun. We reach the edge of the woods and wait.*

*When the night is black, I ride; hour upon hour do I ride. This night is clear and I watch the stars for a bearing. Sometimes I walk the horse, sometimes it almost seems that she flies. Rising behind me the Moon glows full and high, lighting the way.*

*Ahead I see monolithic rocks rising to the night sky and the mist of ocean reaches all about us. The tang of salt is in the rider's nose and I see my nostrils flare and my eyes widen with that same unseeing passion. We approach the cliffs and I hear the roaring of waves thrashing upon the rocks below as if relentlessly drawing all within themselves. A wild place is this! I see a vast expanse of inky blackness within each rock's shadow, which is also the sea over which the Moon glows, causing a pathway between herself and the things beneath the waters.*

*I stop to light the lantern for the path is rough and the mare troubles with each step. I sigh and lay my head upon my arm before raising myself straight within the saddle. "It is now," I whisper, "We wait and seek no more! As known, I have arrived!" I look ahead to a rocky outcrop like a finger upon the sea.*

*I ride hard then, sparks flying from the horse's hooves upon the granite way. As we approach the peninsula, I see a faint glow, as if from another lantern. I slow down now, and throw my own light over the cliff. I am wary and seek to approach unseen. I dismount and walk toward the glow. I see a small cottage almost buried, so deeply was it built within the overhang of the cliffs, like a tiny fortress against the wild winds and sea. A lonelier spot I have never known.*

*The rider's face is set like stone and I cannot perceive what thoughts are veiled within. We walk with dignity, as if to our death.*

*I come at length to the door, of massive proportion compared to the size of the cottage. I hesitate not but bang a fist upon it, a sigh upon cold lips. There is a wait, then a woman's voice calls from beyond the door, "Who comes?"*

*"I am called (your ritual name)," I shout. There is a laugh from within and the door is swung wide. There stands a small*

*woman dressed in male attire, with wild copper hair cascading
down her back.*

*"You are doubly welcome, (name), and thrice! We have waited
long for you!"*

*"I knew it to be true!" I reply, although I smile not. "Was it you
who called me here?"*

*"It was your own dream, (name), and not of our doing. Enter.
I shall tether the mount and see her well."*

*"What name have you?" I ask, without moving; but she just
smiles and shakes her head and again bids me enter.*

*The room is dark save for the lantern in the window and the
fire in the hearth. I see that only the first of the cottage is man-
hewn and that the rest is of solid rock formed from the depths of
the cliff. A hooded figure stands from a chair beside the fire.
Straight of frame and as tall as an elm, but with the whiteness of
hair to tell of great age, that falls to shoulders that show no stoop,
hallowed with fireglow. He wears a robe of heavy dove-gray
wool, and as he moves toward me he smiles. I see great love in
the smile, but as I look into his eyes I flinch at their blackness
and depths. There is unfathomable power within them as though
they had seen the passing of time from its very conception and
had learned from the travel all that had been there to learn.*

*"I've missed you, (name)! Blessed be!" he says, as though he
knows me well. He takes my arm and leads me to stand before the
fire. "We have known that you would come." He laughs with
obvious glee.*

*"Who is the woman? By all the Gods, who are you?" I demand,
as, although this whole thing excites me, I fear it also and am
tired of the mystery that has haunted me waking and sleeping.*

*"She is who I am, and who you are to become!" he replies.*

*"Her name?"*

*"Call Her (a name from myth with which you resonate), and She will answer you!"*

*"And you, Sir, what be your name?" I ask again.*

*"(The same name from myth) is one of the names that I am known to be, child."*

*"And why am I here?" I ask, hoping for confirmation of my yearning.*

*"To learn, (name), the secrets of life and fire! To be at one with Her and mold tomorrow with all of my yesterdays!" he says.*

*"What must I do?" I ask.*

*"Show me the ritual!"*

—Ly de Angeles

You will return, then, to the place of your circle and proceed with the rite. Refer to your Book of Shadows only if absolutely necessary. Go deosil about your circle and light all the candles, then the incense. Consecrate the water with your athame, making the sign of the pentagram in it. Consecrate the salt, likewise, and add it to the water.

Now stand and, beginning at the gate of Earth, hold aloft your pentacle and bear it about your circle, leaving it at the gate once you have returned there. Do likewise from the gate of Air, with the incense; at the gate of Fire with both the black and the white candles of duality (that you have on the altar); and from the gate of Water with the consecrated water, sprinkling as you walk your circle.

Return to the altar, raise your dagger aloft and say:

> **I, (name), in this place which is not a place,**
> **and in this time which is not a time,**
> **do give my most solemn and sacred oath**
> **that I will abide by my chosen path**
> **and will fulfill the dance of my destiny**
> **without complaint,**
> **knowing it to be the Way of that**
> **which I call my Goddess**
> **and that which I call my God!**
> **I shall keep silent all things**
> **entrusted to me by the Gods**
> **and by those who seek silence of me,**
> **in the true nature of priestess (priest)!**
> **I hereby take upon myself the life of witch**
> **and tell all that gather here**
> **that my name is (name)!**

Now take the pentagram necklace from the altar, go deosil about your circle, and hold it up to each gateway saying:

Earth, I call to you,
great guardian of the gate of Earth!
I hold before you the symbol of my initiation!
Acknowledge me,
for I am, (name),
Priestess (Priest) and witch!

Place it momentarily on the pentacle to infuse it with the power of Earth.

Air, I call to you,
great guardian of the gate of Air!
I hold before you the symbol of my initiation!
Acknowledge me,
for I am (name),
Priestess (Priest) and witch!

Hold the pentacle within the smoke of the incense for a moment to infuse it with the power of Air.

Fire, I call to you,
great guardian of the gate of Fire!
I hold before you the symbol of my initiation!
Acknowledge me,
for I am (name),
Priestess (Priest) and witch!

Pass the amulet through the flames to charge it with the power of Fire.

Water, I call to you,
great guardian of the gate of Water!
I hold before you the symbol of my initiation!
Acknowledge me,
for I am (name),
Priestess (Priest) and witch!

Dip the amulet into the consecrated water to charge it with the power of that element.

Return to your altar and drop the pentacle necklace over your head.

Take up your athame and place the blade, oh, so sensually, into the wine in your chalice and say:

Power and passion, the way of the art;
Lover and lover as Goddess and God,
United and blessed, the blood of the vine,
Cup and athame cojoined through desire!

Sip. Put a drop of this fluid on your finger and trace the pentagram on your own forehead with it.

Stand and take the vial of sacred oil. Put a little on both of your feet saying,

Blessed be these feet
made to walk the path of the twice-born!

Touch your knees with the oil saying:

Blessed be these knees
made to kneel at the altar of all things!

Touch your genitals with the oil saying:

**Blessed be the way of the creation of life!**

Touch oil to your chest saying:

**Blessed be this breast
formed in beauty and strength!**

Touch oil just above and below your lips saying:

**Blessed be these lips that speak the truth;
by all the names of Goddess and God!
May I be blessed! Blessed be!**

Finally you will dedicate yourself to one of the faces of both Goddess and God; name them, understanding that these names represent certain powers and influences that you seek to know and represent. Oath yourself to clarity and the refusal of betrayal of the Way of Witch.

Drink deeply now from the cup, leaving a libation that you will pour onto the earth.

Take up your athame and circle from Earth to Air to Fire to Water, farewelling each guardian and closing each gate.

Write in the back of your *Book of Shadows* the ritual name that you have taken and the date of your initiation (and any other pertinent details).

Then open your circle using your athame to withdraw the force field; earth it as you have been taught. Put away all things of ritual.

Have a feast to ground yourself and celebrate.

The rite is done. Blessed be!

Before you go to sleep that night, and each night for a couple of weeks, repeat silently, or whispered, using your ritual name:

**I am (name),
Priestess (Priest) and witch.**

# Section Three

# SECOND STAGE TECHNIQUE PROGRESSIVE

his next section deals with what you might not consider logical, or even rational. These are techniques that presuppose your progress and your study and your experience of the exercises given thus far. These projects are early experiments into the more mystical elements of magical practice; we will then progress to the many specific techniques of sorcery.

## REALMS OF ACCESSIBILITY

By "realms of accessibility" I mean realms or places that are other than physical. They are not perceived by the five senses at the perimeter of your circle, but are accessed only (through the tool of imagery) by the doorway of your center. None of the techniques require any form of mind-altering substances, and will be accessible if you have utilized true inner control. There are several books available that give pathworkings in detail; however, I prefer to provide the setting and the framework and let you freefall within these parameters.

The first technique requires a sound practical meditative background and a strong ability to work deep visualization. This exercise is practiced in various representations by almost all mystery schools of the occult. You may find it useful to actually tape the voyages after reading them, and prior to your experience of them, but they are best consigned to memory.

There are ten realms that you will travel; the first realm has four initial phases through which you will pass *before* proceeding to the others. The last three realms are not to be accessed without having traveled all others in succession, due to the intensity of their intent.

The following exercise is one of freefalling through the Sephiroth of the Tree of Life on a journey inward to the roots of the tree, and of the Seven Planes of Existence, in symbol.

## Exercise

Take the position you have become accustomed to for the meditation and visualization exercises. Employ either active or passive silence. Begin with meditation, taking yourself as deeply as possible without losing conscious control. Take your time.

Begin your visualization by seeing the outside of your circle.

## First Realm: The Four Parts of the Self

Visualize within that circle a vast expanse of black, empty space. In that space are countless millions of miles of sheer velvety blackness, but way past that is a speck of light. Travel toward the light. On your way, you will pass many floating objects created to delude you into thinking you are not going where you will yourself. Destination: speck of light. These objects will consist of anything from chairs, tables, houses, and people to scientific equations, mathematical formulae, and quotations from books. They may be anything that your five outer senses could perceive.

What you are doing is passing through the dimension of your conscious mind. You need to be aware of this in the background of your voyage because at this stage you are still within the first part of the first realm. Continue the voyage until you reach the point of light in the distance. See it, as you approach, as a vast illumined portal that you are to pass through.

When you have passed through the portal, you will find yourself standing on stone steps. Around you as far as you can see there is a boundless expanse of water. The only way to progress is to go in the water and merge with it. Dive into the water and look around. Begin to move forward. Become like a swift current in the water. Be observant at all times; however, don't allow anything you see to deter you from your journey. After traveling thus for a while, observe a portal in the distance. Travel toward the portal. When you reach it, go through it.

When you have passed through the portal, you will find yourself bathed in brilliant light. There are massive pillars that form a corridor; the pillars to your left are black and the pillars to your right are white. They shine like polished marble. You can see nothing but the path beneath your feet due to the brilliance of the light around you. Follow the path. You will hear a loud, continuous, roaring sound (like a huge grindstone turning slowly at the bottom of a deep well). The path you walk on leads you toward the sound. After having traveled thus for a time, you see ahead of you the source of the sound; you see a huge vortex or whirlpool.

As you enter the vortex, your initial sensation is of falling and spinning down a vast chasm. The roaring sound is all around you and you can do nothing but let the falling take you deeper and deeper down into the vortex. Experience the sensation of falling, falling. You need have no fear as you are now traveling through the doorway of your own center; through the doorway of existence. You will eventually land in a small chamber that has only one door; engraved into it is a circle with an equal-arm cross. You are to open the door and pass through.

## Second Realm: Astral

You are in deep night. The landscape is desolate and barren, but beautiful in its moonlit, misty austerity. You can see, by the strong light of the Moon's glow, a path beneath your feet that winds off into the distance leading toward a mountain of rock. You walk the path. Observe everything as you travel toward the mountain. The path ends at the base of the rock, and built into the face of the rock is a pale, wooden door with a thin lunar crescent (☽), made of silver, set into it. You knock on the door and wait. It is opened from the other side. This is the Gate of Moon—the doorway that is the entrance to most inner-plane encounters.

The door is opened by a small woman with dark hair, mysterious and veiled, and swathed in violet robes. She is the guardian of the Moon gate. She says nothing to you until you have passed into the mountain of rock. You enter and she tells you to make the journey alone. You go on your way for a while, observing everything.

When you have wandered through this mountain and found whatever information or knowledge that is significant to you there, the little, dark-haired woman appears again and guides you to the next door. This door is the color of the rising sun and has the symbol of Mercury (☿) carved into it. It shimmers with liquid mercury. You knock on the door and wait until it is opened from the other side.

### Third Realm: First Inner Plane

The door is opened by the guardian of this gate—a being robed in orange, intelligent and alert of visage. The entire place that you have just accessed is diffused with a deep red glow. The guardian who opened the door is more female than male, but is definitely a mixture of both. This being is both the master and servant of this realm, and as you move through this place, you are to observe and listen to everything. You are accompanied by the guardian, who will either tell you and show you many things, or may choose to tell and show you nothing, leaving you to your own devices. Just flow with whatever happens until you are shown to the next door.

This door is the color of a wooded glade and has the symbol of Venus ($♀$) carved into its surface, set with copper. You knock and wait until it is opened from the other side.

### Fourth Realm: Second Inner Plane

The guardian who opens the door is sensual and earthy, robed in emerald green. The entire environment is lit by a deep orange/amber glow. The being who opened the door is more male than female, but is definitely a mixture of both. This being is both the master and the servant of this realm, and as you move through this domain, you are to observe and listen to everything. The guardian accompanies you and chooses to either tell and show you what is there to be known, or leaves you to find out for yourself. Flow with whatever occurs until the guardian takes you to the next door.

This door is the color of the sun at midday and has the glyph of the Sun ($☉$) carved into its face, set with gold. You knock, as before, and await its opening from the other side.

## Fifth Realm: Third Inner Plane

The door is opened by its guardian, glorious and noble, robed in saffron garments. The place is a haze of yellow. The guardian is androgynous. This being is both the master and the servant of this realm, and as you travel through it, you are to observe and listen to everything. The guardian will accompany you, and may choose to impart much that is important to the furtherance of your quest, or may leave you to your own devices. Flow with whatever occurs. When your time here is done, you are guided to the next portal.

This door is the color of blood and has the sign of Mars ($\male$) carved into its face, set with iron. You knock and wait.

## Sixth Realm: Fourth Inner Plane

The door is opened by the guardian of the sixth realm—a being robed in scarlet with a visage savage, clear, and powerful. All within this place is cast in a deep green haze. The guardian is more female than male, but is definitely a mixture of both. This being is the master and the servant of this realm, and will accompany you through it. The guardian has the right to either show you what is important here or to leave you to discover those things on your own. No matter what happens, flow with the experience until the guardian takes you to the door of the next realm.

This door is the blue of a tropical lagoon and has the sign of Jupiter ($\jupiter$), cast in tin, set within its surface. You knock and wait.

## Seventh Realm: Fifth Inner Plane

The door is opened by its guardian, robed in sapphire blue, its visage wise and compassionate. The fifth inner plane is awash with crystal-blue light. The guardian is more male than female, but is a sure mixture of both. Master and servant of this realm, the guardian who accompanies you chooses whether or not to communicate with you. If you are left to your own devices, you are to remember everything you observe on the journey through this place. Flow with the experience until the guardian leads you to the door of the next realm.

This door is as black as obsidian, the sign of Saturn (♄), set in lead, hinting at the force you are yet to encounter. Knock and wait until the door is opened from the other side.

## Eighth Realm: Sixth Inner Plane

No one opens the door, but the door opens just the same. The atmosphere of this realm is thick with the glow of purple. Ahead of you is a fissure in the far wall leading to a narrow passageway down which you will proceed. The destination of the passage is a vast cavern that has been cut from the bedrock of the mountain by unknown forces. The purple glow is all around you.

At the end of the cavern, a woman, dressed in diaphanous black robes that glitter with jewels of jet, is seated on a throne that has been intricately carved from the cavern rock. She is veiled. There is a large silver disc set into the floor before the throne, upon which are engraved the pentagram of the art and seals and sigils inscrutable to you at this point in your quest. You are to approach her and sit down on the silver disc. She either will, or will not, speak with you, but she is capable of projecting images and concepts directly into your mind, which you would do well to heed. *Forget nothing!*

She is the guardian of this realm and *image* of the Queen of the Deep, Goddess of the Underworld.

There is no servant here. She is mistress of this realm.

When it's time for you to leave, she points to a door in the wall of the cavern. This door is the color of the stars; too bright to see the seal of Uranus (⛢) glowing at its center, cast in metal of white fire. You knock on this door and it opens of its own volition.

## Ninth Realm: Seventh Inner Plane

This realm is diffused with a glow that is as white as pearl and has the same sheens. Again there is a passageway that leads you to a bright, bright cavern with many high-arched windows that look out onto more whiteness. The pearly glow is everywhere.

There is a man enthroned in the place, garbed in white with a harlequin mask covering the upper half of his face. His robes are adorned with the signs of the zodiac. At the foot of his seat is a wide, gold disc, lying flat on the floor, the face of which is engraved with the caduceus, the signs of the zodiac, the planets known to us, and the glyphs of the four elements in the signs of the Chayoth ha-Qadesh (the four Holy Living Creatures: winged lion, winged bull, eagle, and angel). You walk forward and seat yourself on its face.

He may or may not use language to communicate with you, being capable, as was the woman, of projecting directly into your consciousness those things that he wants you to know. *Forget nothing that you come to realize.*

There is no servant here. He is master of this realm and the *image* of the God of Light.

Upon completion of your union with this realm, he will direct you toward the way through the final point that you will pass on this journey. It's not a door, but a portal, swirling with hints of all the other colors that you have passed through; more like a veil of the possibility of color than actual color itself. You have simply to walk through; no one bars the way.

## Tenth Realm: Akasha—Hall of Records

You enter into an eternal space that is of no color, simply swirling luminescence. As far as you can see or sense in any direction, there are spheres that can be entered and experienced for whatever treasure they hold. They are suspended by the force of their own energy.

Within each of these spheres is a vast library of knowledge that stretches from infinity to infinity; all that is, was, and is yet to be is contained here. Who knows? You may enter one of these spheres and discover all pertinent information directly influencing your eternally waking soul! But that's for another journey.

Now it's appropriate that you leave. To do so, all you do is turn around (wherever you are standing), and you will find a vortex into which you will project yourself. The vortex will carry you back to the outside of your circle and into the world, where your body awaits you.

You can make this journey a thousand times and not receive the same information from any one realm. You can enter any realm through the vortex after accessing the Gate of Moon, *except* the last three, as these realms are the *result* of a journey through all the rest and accessing the answers they have for you.

The guidelines are specific—it is pointless doing this exercise unless you adhere to them. When you have completed your travels, you are to record all pertinent information in your grimoir. Don't seek to analyze the experience in a logical sense. Just acknowledge it and be willing to accept it for now. During the days following your working, observe the events that occur that are pertinent to the experiences of the inner planes.

## RELEVANT NOTES ON QABBALAH

There is no reason for me to introduce you to either the ceremonial or magickal (a term coined by A. Crowley to distinguish ritual magic from the public's idea of stage conjuring) significance of Qabbalah, as it is not my concern here; however, a basic knowledge of this extraordinary system is relevant as a way of understanding both the self and *how* events actualize.

Qabbalah is also known as Kabbala, Kabbalah, the Tree of Life, Otz Chim, the Ladder of Lights, the Asherah Tree, QBL, and Qbblh. It has been expounded on as both a mystical Hebraic system of comprehending the "body of God," and the soul of Adam Kadmon since, specifically, Moses de Leon introduced the Zohar to the West in the thirteenth century. It can be recognized in the biblical Old Testament in writings from the Pentateuch to the Book of Ezekiel, but it can also be seen, previous to this, in the ancient texts of the legends of Sumer, where it was known as the Ladder of Lights. It is commonly called "the Tree" amongst practitioners of the occult. It is interesting to note just how many of the legends of ancient people resonated with the Tree—from the Druids of ancient Britain to the Norse legends of Yggdrasil.

To expand your understanding, I am quoting here from *An Illustrated Encyclopedia of Traditional Symbols* by J. C. Cooper, (p. 176).

> **Tree.** The whole of manifestation; the synthesis of heaven, earth and water; dynamic life as opposed to the static life of the stone. Both an imago mundi and axis mundi, the "Tree in the midst" joining the three worlds and making communication between them possible, also giving access to a solar power; an omphalos; a world center. The tree also symbolizes the feminine principle, the nourishing, sheltering, protecting, supporting aspect

of the Great Mother, the matrix and the power of the inexhaustible and fertilizing waters she controls; trees are often depicted in the style of a female figure. Rooted in the depths of the earth, at the world center, and in contact with the waters, the tree grows into the world of Time, adding rings to manifest its age, and its branches reach the heavens and eternity and also symbolize differentiation on the plane of manifestation.

The Tree is considered sacred in Celtic, Chinese, Christian, Egyptian, Graeco-Roman, Hebrew, Hindu, Iranian, Islamic, Japanese, Mexican, Mithraic, Scandinavian, Sumero-Semetic, Taoist, Teutonic, Australian Aboriginal, Buddhist, and Druidic traditions. The Tree was considered sacred to Asherah, Attis, Dionysis/Bacchus, Woden, Atargatis, Odin, Cybele, Esus, Kentigern, Yeheshuah, Hathor, Osiris, Zeus/Jupiter, Apollo, Artemis, Karuatis, Adonis, Heracles/Hercules, Daphne, Silvanus, Pan, God (with its ten emanatory names), Brahman, Aditi/Diti, Zoroaster, Allah, Ashtoreth, Astarte, and likely many, many others.

My notions pertinent to the Tree are heretical from the viewpoint of both the religious perspective relative to the subject and the ways and practices of Qabbalists (who also call their tradition High Magick). For this I make no apology.

The above is a matter for contemplation. The magical workings are the offspring of the previous techniques you have accessed and the profundity available through understanding the following information.

# THE TREE

There are three factors to be understood:

1.  The Glyph of the Tree, as it manifests from its seed (Kether) to its realization (Malkuth), through the cycle of its own becoming (from the pattern of itself inherent in the seed to the fruit within which the same seed perpetuates itself through reproduction, ad infinitum). The tree *is immanence,* which is why it represents eternal life.

2.  The Body of the Tree (known as Nephesh—body, Ruach—soul, Neschamah—spirit); also called Adam Kadmon (or Eternal Tribe). The Body of the Tree tells us of the *way* of self-realization.

3.  The Worlds (four) of the Tree tell us *the way of manifestation*; tell us *how time happens*; tell us the laws of actualization (in alignment with the Law of Congruity).

It's all within the pattern, you see? The outcome to any scenario is inherent within it! It's always seed to root, to leaf, to stem, to flower to fruit . . . to seed, do you see?

# THE GLYPH

1.  Each of the circles of the glyph are known as spheres.

2.  Collectively, these spheres are called Sephiroth; singularly they are called Sephirah.

3.  There are ten objective Sephiroth and one subjective Sephirah (known as Da'ath).

4.  The Sephiroth are also paths.

5.  The twenty-two obvious paths that link the Sephiroth (there are infinite paths that are not obvious) are also the Major Arcanum of the Tarot.

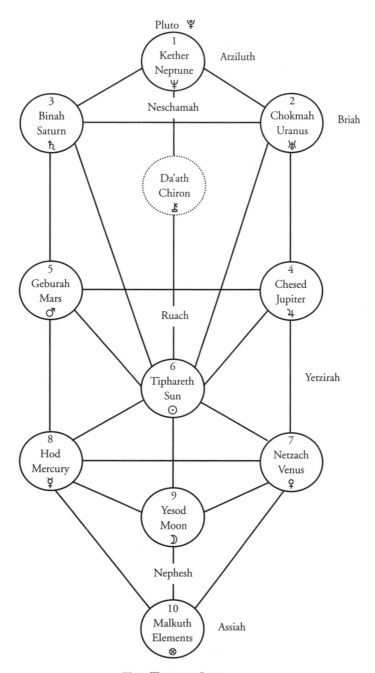

THE TREE OF LIFE

6. The planets of our known zodiac are the manifest expressions of the Tree (the Tree, then, is also a star map), and the qualities of the planets are relative to the qualities of an individual, a society, a culture. Their balance or imbalance being understood via an understanding of these qualities.

7. The Tree is seen as a grouping of separate entities, and is evaluated by the qualities of those separate entities, but, like a tree in the forest, it is all one Tree, indivisible and complete. Therefore, the Sephiroth are to be understood as *unfolding* from Kether to Malkuth along a recognizable line known as the Lightning Flash (also represented by the serpent, Nehushtan).

8. The Tree also represents an understanding of the concept of evolution, seemingly in reverse (i.e., we seem to progress from primitive to refined, *but* life doesn't go in a straight line!), in the way of the big bang theory insofar as what we are becoming (like light expanding instantaneously from an unrecognizable point to wherever it is) *is* what we have always been, but we are becoming through the experience of material reality, and we know this—it is inherent in the atomic field, and deeper still, in each and every thing—the knowledge of such is simply not cognitive, and therefore, not understood by way of *conscious* pathways; but the pattern of the Tree tells the story (i.e., from seed to fruit ad infinitum).

The further we explore the frontiers of science (see *The Death of Forever* and *Music of the Mind* by D. Reanney, and *Chaos* by J. Gleick) through such fields as quantum physics and chaos theory, the more obvious the complexity and viability of much that is considered ancient wisdom.

The concepts inherent in the theory of the Tree, in its infinitude, are reflected in the weirdness and profundity of the Benoit

B. Mendelbrot set as seen in both *Chaos* and Mendelbrot's own text called *Fractal Geometry of Nature.*

# THE DIVISIONS OF THE SOUL
# (THE BODY OF THE TREE)

1. Neschamah is the triad of Kether, Chokmah, and Binah. It is called "spirit" and it is the predetermination factor immanent in both awareness (soul: Ruach) and manifestation (body: Nephesh). Neschamah could be considered the pattern of both destiny (on an individual level) and evolution (collectively). Kether is immanence; Chokmah is force (realizing an uncontained energetic principle), and Binah is form (energy coherent within measurable parameters, or time).

One could postulate, then, that there is no free choice if the pattern is already set, but varying factors will always determine the presentation of experience. Life rejoices in diversity. Magically, it is the clarity of choices that determine the quality of future experience. Manifestation is malleable, dependent on the vessel through which an experience is summoned. Therefore . . .

2. The Ruach, called "the soul," is the awareness of individuality interrelative to experience. It includes (in order of the Lightning Flash) Chesed, Geburah, Tiphareth, Netzach, Hod, and Yesod.

What does this mean? Consider yourself to be Tiphareth (Sun), and that you are central to everything you experience, think, do, and express (and, of course, by the very fact that you *are*, all things are experienced by you!). The nature of the Sephiroth revolving and swirling around you will mirror themselves in your day-to-day living and will be reflections of who you are because all experiences are *perceptions* of reality rather than whatever reality may or may not actually be (take light, for example; we see only a minute fraction of the actual spectrum of light—all else concerned with light is vibratory, or wavelike, and requires other factors to enable us to interpret it—this is so with all reality).

Your ability to be clear about what you *do* perceive as reality, and your participation within it, is what practical magic is reliant on (see Section One). Therefore, to seek to know the nature of experience, we use a framework of recognizable parameters (like the nature of the planets and all else relative to the Sephiroth) and to eradicate dysfunction. The *primary* way of doing this is to know your own nature. *Life will mirror it!* That's the Law of Congruity, and future seeds will integrate the information (bearing in mind that death is part of the cycle of all things and can occur many, many times in the course of one apparent lifetime. The seeds of how you live are the determining factor of the future lives of the Tree (individually).

3.  Nephesh is both the stage on which life presents its unfolding drama, and material reality, as we know it, personally and collectively. It is the domain whereby that which is conceived in Neschamah is fulfilled. It could, therefore, be considered the outcome of life (i.e., Death . . . life . . . death . . . life . . . death . . . life. Death in this frame of reference being understood as transformative). Creation continuous!

4.  The symbol of the "Divisions of the Soul" is, therefore, a circle.

# THE FOUR WORLDS

The Tree of Life is divided into four aspects:

1. Atziluth indicates Kether.

2. Briah includes Chokmah and Binah.

3. Yetzirah includes Chesed, Geburah, Tiphareth, Netzach, Hod, and Yesod.

4. Assiah indicates Malkuth.

It is to be understood that there is a tree in each Sephirah; there are four worlds to each and every tree. There are, upon initial consideration, therefore, four hundred trees to the Tree of Life—it ends up seeming like an infinite stairwell with each landing leading elsewhere, representing one or another of the Sephiroth, except that the stairwells lead in every direction. Hence, not just the *Tree* of Life but the Tree of *Life!* Boundless possibilities and realities all intersecting—get the picture?

I'll keep this as concise as possible. You are to consider the four worlds in accordance with two principles: (1) the essential four worlds and (2) the process of creation and time. To cause an event or phenomenon to occur (manifestation implies time, as it implies actualization), it is necessary to comprehend the principles of creation in the first place, *and creation requires reciprocation!*

# The Essential Four Worlds

Malkuth is the *only* Sephirah in the world of Assiah, but there is a Tree in Malkuth. This is our concern here: to access the four worlds *through* Assiah, therefore *consciously* linking Assiah to and within the other worlds.

**Atziluth** is archetypal, divine. It is the principle of the qualities of Air; realized as inspiration. Its symbol is the sword.

**Briah** is creative, archangelic. It is the principle of the qualities of Fire; realized as excitation. Its symbol is the staff.

**Yetzirah** is formative, angelic. It is the principle of the qualities of Water; realized as emotion. Its symbol is the chalice.

**Assiah** is active, the material universe. It is the principle of the qualities of Earth; realized as *manifestation*. Its symbol is the pentacle.

# THE PRINCIPLE OF CREATION

This process requires reciprocation, mutual accord. To understand this, it is necessary to consciously remove the idea that humanity is a supreme facet of creation, and to concede that we are a facet of creation; our intelligence, our reasoning capabilities, our feelings, and our foibles are in accordance with the principles of creation; not distinct from all else, but in relativity to all else. You've got to get this idea so that you *can* actualize things.

## Example

One day I am struck with an idea (Atziluth) that springs from a need: I want to make a special box to keep my valuable ritual things away from others' eyes. To make my box, I will need particular ingredients, like the wood, maybe glue, hammer, nails or screws, a screwdriver, ruler, saw, pencil perhaps, hinges, and paper for drawing up a plan.

Resulting from the idea is a blueprint; I design my box (Briah).

It is necessary for me to then assess my resources, gather the ingredients, and implement the determination and effort (Yetzirah) necessary for me to assure the desired outcome. If I have followed certain guidelines, I will have my box (Assiah).

That all sounds very simple, doesn't it? It *is*, if the box is simple, if the equipment is readily available, if I have an understanding of the mathematical conditions necessary for box-making, and if the ingredients are willing.

Did she say ". . . if the ingredients are willing?"

Consider the wood (we'll leave out the other things, but you'll know what I am aiming at if you've ever had trouble with even one nail!): a piece of wood is something on the way to becoming something else (just like a hydrogen atom was, at one point). At some phase of its progression, it was probably a tree; before it was a tree it was a seed . . . backwards through time to when it was nothing of the sort. Through random selection or perfect design, it became that which is now recognizable as wood. I add that wood to an overall grouping of objects and it reciprocates by considering them worthy companions for the interim term of its journey as "box." Three billion light years from now, will it possibly retain that memory?

Three billion light years from the time I was other than what I am now, did I understand the nature of wood, when it was other than wood? Chances are, the answer to that is yes.

Reciprocation requires both time and energy—*that* is the principle of the four worlds! Sympathetic magic requires that you understand this: that to effect an outcome, you must be in sympathy with the process. It makes it all so easy.

## TIME AND THE FOUR WORLDS

Time doesn't exist in a straight line, that's for sure, but it is perceived that way. The symbol of eternity is ∞, but this symbol is not shown here in three dimensions and can, therefore, be misleading on the one hand and correct on the other.

The crossover point between the two circles is like Assiah—it's where we are right now. The furthest distance from the crossover point, on either circle, is Atziluth. The journey between the crossover point and the furthest distance is the intermeshing process of Yetzirah and Briah. The two opposing furthest distances are mirror images of each other. One furthest distance could be considered as the past, one could be considered the future; one of the furthest distances could be microcosmic, the other macrocosmic. Assiah is the ever-happening "now." What is interesting, however, is that in three dimensions we see:

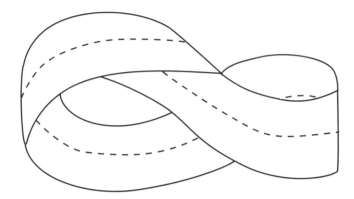

The Möbius Veil

A Möbius strip (on the Tree it is considered the veil that sepa-
rates Neschamah and that which is above the abyss, from the rest
of the Tree, or that which is below the abyss) is one circle with a
twist. The circle has two faces and two sides—it represents duality in all its guises, always being only one thing (i.e., the circle
with its twist). The twist is time, it causes us think that we are
not participating in tomorrow when we are! The twist is there so
that life can never underestimate its own next trick; but it's all
there. Everything that was, is, and ever will be.

Time is a tool invented by us to help us (1) gauge the age of a
thing, (2) plan, (3) measure the distance from one aspect of the
cycles and the seasons to another, and (4) attempt to render
finite that which is understood by way of its currently perceived
state of reality. We are *not* governed by it, controlled by it, or in
any way degraded by it. Time is manifest eternity! So that one
could say that Atziluth is the pattern of now (Assiah) that is
only recognized retrospectively, and that the process of getting
to that retrospective state (memory or reflection concerning the
past), which is Yetzirah and Briah inclusively, is the modus
operandi of creation.

The simple fact that we can make anything at all assures us of our participation in the process of creation—we are reciprocal to the process.

Therefore, the very conscious idea of spellcrafting has Atziluth as its parent, seed, and source, and Assiah as its essential outcome!

# Part Three

## SPELLCRAFTING (SORCERY)

## Binah
## No. IV

Love is in detachment from the strings that end up tying tighter than love was ever meant to be. Love without fear of what may come tomorrow—for that is what love is. It belongs to no one but yourself and cannot be taken or given as a token or a gift. Your worries and fears have nothing to do with love—they are extensions of either the world around you, or your own shortcomings. Compare them not to love or you will lose your choice in the matter of love . . .

. . . and if love be not free and exhilarating then it is not love but demand and desire for possession of that which you are not.

Love allows.

It is not reactive,

It is a perspective of self—self in reflection and glory, mirrored in a feeling that is beautiful to feel

. . . anything else is not love, but obligation . . .

and that is something else to be worked with.

The Moon in you and you and you and you . . .

The Moon in you belongs right where it is or it would not be there!

Child, it is all in the perspective.

—from *The Feast of Flesh & Spirit* by Ly de Angeles

# Section One

# APPLICATION

## LETTING GO

Now, you've got to let it go; all of it. Everything within you that is tame. This section is easy. The ways of making and changing are easy—it all depends on letting go.

Water, wind, air, and earth, stones and sea and stars, "sweat, and softly moan before the fire . . ." Wild places and songs you can't quite catch hold of; things that whisper to you in the night that wake you suddenly . . . and the only reason you don't follow them? Let it go! Others needn't see. Others can continue to know you the way they know you. This is a secret world, the Way of the witch who weaves songs into actuality; a secret way that you may have been taught, sometime, by someone, "is only for the children, or the truly mad!" It's a fine line we walk; that's why so many of us are deemed weird . . . but where's the madness in wonder?

I'm awake at dawn. I've been awake for hours. The deep night called my name, woke me up, said, "Think, Ly!" So I did . . . for hours. The sun will be up soon, but right now the ravens call and I can hear the way the day will go by the way I know our song. The magpies tell that it will rain today; I wish it wouldn't because I love the sun, but they're always right, just like the plovers.

That's the first way to know about making things happen. You've got to walk the way of the wild things, because humans tend to force things, to twist things around, to want so much that they forget that it's all just *out there*. Like making the box, in the last section, magic is all about knowing that what will happen *wants to happen!*

. . . and if the magic believes in you, how can you not answer its ancient call?

So, what I'm *not* going to do in this final section is provide you with a recipe book. I will give information and instruction pertinent to the techniques. The fine print, and the artistry, will depend on your needs.

## FITH-FATHING

This is one of the best enchantments that you can use to acquire or affect—anything. A fith-fath is also called a poppet or a dolly, though it doesn't always look figure-like unless your spell is specifically aimed at affecting another person. We'll begin, however, with the person thing.

You'll want to create a likeness, be it from cloth that's stuffed with appropriate materials and sewn (by hand!), or from clay or wax molded to form. You'll want it sympathetic to its likeness, so bits of the likeness, or photographic images, are to be acquired whenever possible and added to the fith-fath.

Whether you are drawing the human likeness *to* you, binding it from causing harm, assisting it in deciding an outcome in your favor, or performing a healing, you are going to need to give it life.

You'll want to have all requirements gathered and to work your sorcery in a well-cast circle. You *won't* tell anyone of your work (but I've said that enough, by now, so I'm sure you've got the message!). Everything about the making is to be felt; be aware of every emotion and keep the reason for fith-fathing foremost in your thoughts.

One of the most seductive ways of working this spell is to create a short, but pertinent, rhyme—just a four-liner—repeat the rhyme over and over in a monotonous rhythm until you lose the words and simply end up making a hum (to the same rhythm).

You sit. You rock. You make.

When you've completed the making, you will breathe it alive; you will tell it what you want, not just with soft words, but with physical interaction (depending on the intent!). For example, should you desire to prevent a violent person from perpetuating their dysfunction, you will bind them with colored cord (I'm oath-bound not to give you the exact colors, but for a binding of this kind, needless to say, the cord won't be pink!). For a healing, you will fill the fith-fath with specific herbs or healing aids, or you will soothe the desperate spirit if the person's destiny is to experience body-death. By now, you've trained well enough and long enough to be able to focus your intention *without effort.* Understand that if the working requires effort, then the symmetry is not achieved. Once the spell is done, you will put the fith-fath in an extremely appropriate place, one you will have arranged beforehand.

*Warning:* With all sorcery there is risk, so you are to be very sure of why you are doing what you are doing, and don't do it very often unless it becomes your forte. Be wary of meddling.

## Example of Fith-Fathing

You have just been informed by a close friend that her teenage son has been given free tastes of smack (heroin) by a well-known, respected member of the local community. The son of your friend became disturbed when *his* friend, who had also been given free tastes, began needing money when the man informed him that if he desired more he would need to pay. The stirrings of desperation in his friend's developing addiction was what led the son of your friend to inform his mother. The boy says he refuses to talk to police. Worried about consequences, she has come to you. What do you do to help her?

If you know of the man but cannot get anything belonging to him, then his image within your mind will be enough. If you do not know the man, you will need the boy's complicity. It is enough that he can imagine the man's face, his voice, his actions, his clothing, his size, age, hair, skin, eye color, any and all distinguishing features. The mother will need to have the boy write a description, and his feelings about the man. Details are significant.

Preparation for the rite (note that when it is required that you call upon the names of the Lady and Lord, you call upon those names to which you are personally attuned).

First, reive as you have learned. Have all things for the making of the fith-fath in readiness for the rite.

## Requirements for the Rite

Set on your altar the altar candle in its holder, salt and water in their containers, your athame and your pentacle, incense, charcoal blocks and censer, thread to bind the fith-fath, and the chant you have prepared for the rite. Set the candles and candleholders at the elemental gates. Surround your workspace with your white cord. Have matches or a lighter within the space, and the ingredients for the fith-fath. Robe if desired, but this (as are most solitary rites) is best done skyclad.

# THE RITE

Cast the cord around the perimeter of the circle and place the elemental candles at each of the compass points.

Seat yourself before the altar and light the altar candle and the charcoal blocks, placing a small amount of prepared incense on them when they are fully burning.

Center yourself as you have learned to do. When your mind is clear and you are focused clearly on your undertaking, stand, take your athame in your hand, and cast a circle around the boundary of the cord, beginning and ending at the Gate of Earth.

Return to the altar and consecrate the salt by placing the point of your athame into it and saying:

> **Blessed salt, crystal of the sea,**
> **I summon your power to cleanse and guard.**
> **By Earth, by Sky, by Sea,**
> **as I do Will, so mote it be!**

Place the container back on the altar and take up the container of water. Place the tip of your athame into it and say:

> **By my Will I cast out of you all that is unclean!**
> **You are Water, pure clear Water;**
> **I seek your power to aid me in this rite.**
> **By Earth, by Sky by Sea,**
> **as I do Will, so mote it be!**

Add the salt to the water and mix them with the tip of your athame. Stand and cast about your circle with the consecrated water, beginning and ending at the gate of Earth.

Return the container to the altar. Take your wand in one hand and the altar candle in the other, and summon the guardians of each element.

With the altar candle, light the candle at the gate of Earth, and then place it on the ground near you. Raise your wand aloft as you say:

**I summon the protection of the forces of Earth
to guard me and aid me in this rite!
By Aradia and by Cernunnos do I call you here!**

Using your wand, inscribe the invoking pentagram of Earth in the air before you. Sense the guardians before you proceed, with the altar candle, to the gate of Air.

Light the candle at the gate of Air, from the altar candle, which you will then place on the ground near you. Raise your wand aloft as you say:

**I summon the protection of the forces of Air
to guard me and aid me in this rite!
By Aradia and Cernunnos do I call you here!**

Use your wand to inscribe the invoking pentagram of Air before you. Know that the guardians have come before proceeding to the gate of Fire.

Light the candle as before, raise your wand aloft, and say:

**I summon the protection of the forces of Fire
to guard me and aid me in this rite.
By Aradia and Cernunnos do I call you here!**

Use your wand to inscribe the invoking pentagram of Fire.
When the guardians have come, take the altar candle and pro-
ceed to the gate of Water.
Light the candle and raise your wand, saying:

**I summon the protections of the forces of Water
to guard me and aid me in this rite.
By Aradia and Cernunnos do I call you here!**

Wait until the guardians have come before returning to the
altar and replacing the candle thereon. Refuel the censer.

Center yourself again, and prepare yourself to be a vessel for
the power of magic to flow through you and into the fith-fath.
Raise up your athame and call on your Lady and Lord to add
their power to the intent.

**Aradia, Queen of all witches,
lend your power to my spell!
Cernunnos, Lord of the Wild,
lend your power to my spell!
Lady and Lord of Life and Death
lend your power to halt the harm!
Assist me to bind the one who seduces the gullible.
Do as you Will where he is concerned.
By my actions we seal him in!**

Place your athame on the altar. Breathe the power of the Lady
and Lord into yourself. Breathe deeply and exhale fully a number
of times until you feel your hands tingle slightly. Allow your
breathing to become a repetitive hum. Hold this wordless chant
as you make the fith-fath. Allow your mind to consider the circumstances that have induced this spell. Don't invent emotion,

simply be aware and feel freely. When you have made the pop-pet, refuel the censer.

Place the fith-fath on the pentacle, hold the blade of your athame over it, and draw an invoking pentagram of Earth saying:

**Infused of Earth so flesh you are!**

Pass the fith-fath through the incense, hold the blade of your athame over it, and draw the invoking pentagram of Air saying:

**Infused of Air so think you can!**

Pass the fith-fath through the flame of the altar candle, hold the blade of your athame over it, and draw the invoking penta-gram of Fire saying:

**Infused of Fire, choose you can!**

Sprinkle the fith-fath with the consecrated water. Hold the point of your athame over it, and draw the invoking pentagram of Water saying:

**Infused of Water for feeling and sense!**

Lift the fith-fath to your mouth and breathe on it three times with the breath of life, then begin to bind the figure with the thread chanting your rhyme. An example of this rhyme:

**You do not harm,**
**you now will find another way of living.**
**As this cord does bind, you change your mind;**
**not taking now but giving!**

I realize this seems simplistic, but that's what you need it to be. When the fith-fath represents someone who is causing harm, it is always best to summon some form of balancing rather than to cause harm yourself. When you have completed the task, hold the fith-fath aloft saying:

> **By Earth, by Sky by Sea,**
> **By the ancient awesome Law of Three,**
> **The rite is done, so mote it be!**

Immediately put the poppet down, go to the gate of Earth with your wand, thank the forces for attending you, and inscribe the banishing pentagram of Earth in the air before you. Snuff the candle at the gate. Do likewise, using the appropriate banishing pentagrams, at each of the other elemental gates.

Return to your altar and breathe deeply several times to center yourself, saying:

> **Blessed Lady, Lord of the Wild,**
> **I thank you for aiding me.**
> **Take the intent behind the rite**
> **and see it done, so mote it be!**

Open the circle by symbolically cutting the boundary with the blade of your athame. Take up the cord and place it and all other ritual things away. When this is done, put the fith-fath where it will not be disturbed (burying it is sensible) and consciously let it go; forget it. There will be no need to think about it or mention it to anyone.

The rite is done.

## FAMILIARS

Now we're on to one of my favorite things! A familiar is *not* a pet, even though the beast concerned may sleep on your bed or hang from your rafters. The nearest to a pet that a familiar gets is the fact that *sometimes* it will behave like it's domesticated (whatever that's supposed to mean!).

The familiar will always choose you. It will bring you gifts. It will have a life of its own apart from you. What makes it a familiar is its behavior and the simple ability to communicate with you. You can change places in the night (because the night is always the time when the way of a familiar is most blatant) and not be disturbed when you arise in the morning with twigs in your hair and scratches along your shoulders!

A familiar can come and go from a circle *without breaking the seal.* They are messengers and spies and companions for life. Even after the body-death of one of my familiars, he has continued to be useful, stalking the boundary of my property as a barely recognizable entity.

## FETCHES

You make a fetch (like you make a fith-fath), but they are not a representative of humanity and they are *most definitely* to be unmade, once their time is up, for the spell to manifest.

Always make one inside a well-cast circle.

You will gather bits and pieces, like feather and bone and fur and claw, anything that resembles, or has inherent within it, the qualities of your intention. These things are elemental by nature, but fixed in a pattern for a short duration. Your main ingredients are beeswax and string. Beeswax is malleable when it is slightly warm, and your bits can form themselves within and around it. The string, which will be plaited, will bind the spell to its purpose.

A fetch is easier than astral projection, and its aim is to seek and find whatever you desire to come to you. You are to write, on paper, *exactly* what you want. Don't generalize and don't be vague, for again, these tools are not selective; they have no feelings and they have no conscience.

You are to evoke the power of Earth, Air, Water, or Fire (or all) into the fetch bundle and focus on your desire.

Accord a time frame, not more than one month, for the process to be fulfilled. Note that the process is *not* the outcome. The outcome will not occur until the fetch has returned! Think and speak from Moon phase to Moon phase (by week), or from solar cycle to solar cycle (by day). Then send your fetch off to do its job.

## Sample Rite

I desire to draw to me situations that will provide pleasant emotional stimuli. I create a fetch with this intention very clearly rooted in my consciousness. Pleasant emotional stimuli need to feed the heart, mind, and body, therefore I work all four elements into the fetch.

I use dance within the ritual to symbolically represent the desire. I won't focus on any specific outcome, as pleasure is most dynamic when it is both surprising and spontaneous.

## Requirements for the Fetch

1.  The desire, written on a small piece of paper, will be placed within the belly of the fetch.

2.  Earth, when mixed to a paste with oil, is used to empower the fetch and to represent the element of Earth (stimulation of body) when rubbed into the body of the fetch. (In Australia, I can find ochre rock that can be pounded to a powder

as red as blood. As such, is often an integral addition to many of my spells, of both passion and healing.)

3. Beeswax to form what is to be a random shape.

4. Feathers to give the fetch flight and swiftness, and to represent the element of Air (stimulation of mind).

5. Relevant bodily secretions (saliva, sweat, or sexual secretions, depending on the desired outcome) that represent the element of Fire.

6. Water (excitement and emotional stimulation) that you will rub in the belly of the fetch.

7. String for the plaiting of the desire (to charm the spell) which you will also place within the belly of the fetch.

## Requirements for the Ritual

1. The ingredients for the fetch.

2. The appropriate tape or CD (without lyrics), and a player, which you will have with you in your circle.

3. All ritual equipment: chalice (with wine for consecration), athame, wand, pentacle, altar candle, four elemental candles, censer, incense (and charcoal blocks), and matches or lighter.

4. This rite is best worked skyclad.

# THE RITE

Have all things that you require for the rite on your altar and place the elemental candles at each compass point. Light the altar candle.

Using your athame, cast a circle around your work space. Seat yourself before your altar and breathe to quiet the mind.

When you are ready, take up your wand and the altar candle. Go to the gate of Earth, light the candle, raise your wand aloft, and say:

**I call upon the powers of Earth,**
**by Aradia, by Cernunnos!**
**Come to my circle to guard and to guide!**

Draw the invoking pentagram of Earth into the space before you, visualize the gate and the elementals attending, and then say:

**Blessed be the powers of Earth!**

Go around your circle, then, to Air, to Fire, to Water, and summon the powers of each element. Then return the altar candle and your wand to the altar, and light the charcoal. When it is glowing, place incense upon it.

Take your athame and hold it, blade point down, over the chalice of wine. Focus on the understanding of the act of consecration as you lower the blade into the wine saying:

**This Cup is the symbol of Woman and Goddess,**
**this Blade is the symbol of Man and God.**
**Cojoined, are They, in the way of Creation!**
**Life within Death, Death within Life.**
**Blessed be the fruit of the Vine!**

Drink from the cup and sprinkle a few drops on the ground in libation. Put the music on and let yourself go with it in a dance-to-raise-power. Really let yourself go! Dance 'til you drop, aroused with pleasure, at your altar. Wait until your breathing, while still deep from the dancing, becomes regular, then hold your hands, fingers spread, over the makings of your fetch and say:

> **O Lady of Delight, Goddess of Earth and Bounty!**
> **I call upon you by your ancient of Names**
> **Ishtar; Aphrodite; Hecate; Aradia!**
> **Lend me your Power to see the spell done!**
> **O Lord of the Hunt, my God of the Wild-wood!**
> **I call upon you by your ancient of Names**
> **Herne; O great Pan; Cernunnos; Dionysis!**
> **Lend me your Power to see the spell done!**

Feel and sense the powers, thus summoned, flow through you to your fingertips. Knead the beeswax until it is pliant, shaping it into whatever shape is pleasing to your senses, keeping a small cavity open into which you put the written intent and your bodily secretions (leave it open for the moment). Work the earth, that has been mixed to a paste, into the body of the fetch, and then add the feathers.

With your athame, cut the thread into three even lengths, tie them together at one end, place that end between your teeth, and plait the three lengths together while breathing the chant:

> **By the ancient awesome Law of Three;**
> **as I do Will so mote it be!**

Of *course* it won't come out of your mouth sounding like the words! You've got the string between your teeth! It's the sound, the repetition, the intent that is woven into the plait. When the plait is complete, tie off the ends stating the intention of the spell and breathing on it three times. Place the plait into the cavity of the fetch and seal it. Say to the fetch:

**As I make you so I will break you!**
**You have until (state time frame) . . .**
**to fetch my desire**
**only then will my hand set you free!**

Breathe the breathe of life on it and say:

**By Earth, by Sky, by Sea,**
**so be it done, so mote it be!**

Visualize the entity of the fetch flying swiftly from its body as it seeks its purpose.

Refuel the censer, drink a sip of the consecrated wine, raise your athame in one hand and your wand in the other, and give thanks to your lady and lord for their assistance in this rite.

Then, taking your wand only, go to each elemental gateway and give honor and farewell to the guardians gathered there, describing the appropriate banishing pentagram before snuffing each flame. Cut your circle open with your athame and snuff the altar candle saying:

**Blessed be; the rite is done.**

Wrap the fetch in some cloth and place it away with your ritual things until its allotted time.

When the time frame is up, you will summon the entity back into the fetch, from within your circle, break the thing to pieces, and consign the pieces to the earth. Only then will the spell unfold.

You can use this technique to arrange transportation, to get a new vehicle, to have the vehicle you currently own fixed easily if it's broken, to procure money or means when necessity dictates, to aid you in acquiring a holiday or journey, or to provide you with the means to change any unwanted situation in your life . . . after first exhausting all reasonable traditional techniques. Use your capacity to make decisions and choices *first!* Don't run to sorcery for any and every little thing!

Sorcery is worked in synchronicity with summoned sensations, in preference to set outcomes, to enable magic to align life with our desires in accordance with natural laws. It is, however, necessary to image yourself experiencing the achieved outcome (*not* the process).

## SHAPESHIFTING (THERIANTHROPISM)

Shapeshifting is at the heart of most shamanic practice, and it concerns us here because it is a means of travel between places-within-time and other realms of reality.

It is not necessary to work this practice within a cast circle.

You will need to know the heart and soul of the creature(s) you are to become before you undertake the experience. Each of us has the building blocks of all life available at an atomic level, and we are unspecifically connected with all life at the very source of our physiology—the pattern of individual structure is simply the way of art.

Why is it, then, that many of us empathize, at a profoundly deep level, with certain creatures more so than other lifeforms, often even more so than with our own species? With me, it's both the horse and the raven—it's a love affair of the spirit, and merging with the image of either of these creatures is as easy as changing my mind! So I do.

I used to wonder about certain therianthropic creatures, like the Centaur, Pegasus, Abraxis, the Morrigan, and the deities of most polytheistic cultures from Egypt to the Amazon, from the Celts to the Koori, until I realized that they all inferred shapeshifting.

To achieve this state, you can't just take a liking to one or another creature. The understanding is of a deep, deep kinship.

You will require the techniques learned in Part One to take you to the stage of relinquishment necessary to first summon, see, and merge with the form of the creature, and secondly, to *become*, individually, that creature. The process equates to: 1=0=1. Because you are in a state of trance when the process of transformation takes place, there is no way of knowing whether your human form remains at home. Even when I have had others perform the objective-observer role, it's hard to know for sure, as you're not in an ordinary time-synapse when *any* magic is worked.

Shapeshifting is also like riding a medium, in communion with that medium, for whatever reason. It's often done to transport you to a realm for the purpose of learning, or experience, or to bring back a power, but I don't need a reason to do this. The joy of the experience is often enough.

The power of the animal into which one shapeshifts *is not*, please understand, *an outside thing*. My very nature is horselike; my appearance, my very body, is horselike. When I do my physical training, it's with this awareness. My deep-self, my clairvoyance, my very soul is ravenlike—not my appearance, not my attitude. So, there's the three of us already within me, and it's nothing to move from one to the other. It's *natural.*

That's what you've got to know. That's what you've got to realize—not who you are, but *all* of who you are!

Astral projection is a New Age term for the experience of shapeshifting. To leave one form in one place and travel, in another form, to another place, for whatever purpose, was a way of communicating and interacting without distance being a drawback. Now we have technology.

As in the way of the shaman, so in the way of the witch.

Therianthropism is the technical term for shapeshifting. The word is derived from Greek *therion* (wild beast) and *anthropos* (man).

## Exercise

Lie flat on the floor with an appropriate incense and with music that indicates your desired state of consciousness. If you are more at ease within a cast circle, then by all means utilize this skill. You won't need to do any invocations or summonings though.

## Visualization

There is a tunnel-opening at the base of a huge rock, or a particular tree, or a path that leads to a tunnel behind a waterfall. Stand at the entrance and call the shape you desire to manifest from within the tunnel. It will appear in a quasi-solid state. You will move toward it and enter into it. It will merge with you, and your lifeforce will give it solidity. You will travel, then, in that shape, through the tunnel (1) to an archetypal experience for either pleasure or learning; (2) for a healing: to retrieve the essence of an ill person who has been lost (or, sometimes, who has run away from home) during times of crisis or chronic distress or disease; (3) to link with beloveds at a distance; (4) to communicate with someone who has recently died in violent or disturbing circumstances, whose spirit you sense needs assistance for transition; or (5) to read the patterns of truth or lie in the aura of any individual with whom you have dealings, who may seem convincing, but whose motives need to be realized at a core level.

When you have achieved your purpose in that shape, you will return to the tunnel and farewell your image. This can often be an emotional and difficult goodbye, as we become deeply attuned to this ally. Then return to waking consciousness.

Shapeshifting ascertains that you are unrecognizable as your physical persona. You can be much more subtle in your dealings this way *and* more deeply at one with the power of wild-magic.

You will shapeshift into the same form consistently—it tends to become your alter-self. Some may know it's you when the raven or the owl or the dragon lands on the window ledge calling to them loudly, but only if you've told them that this beast may, just possibly, be you!

# GLAMOURING

The danger zone!

Between Mulengro and biology, this is like a bloody nightmare, out of control in our civilized existence because it is generally unconscious and, therefore, uncontrolled. In ancient times, the skill of glamouring was used in a very conscious, magical way to create a desired effect. Whether that effect was to attract or repel depended on the circumstances.

The word *glamour* in contemporary language is commonly used to describe the appearance of certain (mainly) women whose makeup and attire fit a sophisticated, upmarket, fashionable genre, when, really, it stems from an archaic Scottish word *gramayre*, meaning occult lore, magical skill, bewitchment. It is also relative to the word "grammar," hence grimoir, one's personal book of spells! As a tool of bewitchment, it certainly has an effect, even on modern society, seeming to promote an image of wealth and beauty aimed at impressing a particular ideal on the consumer.

Glamouring is an interesting subject, which cross-references with Never to Walk in Anyone's Shadow in Part One. It is advantageous to learn to use glamouring when you *consciously* desire to do so (and to recognize it in others).

Glamouring is the conscious creation of a persona (person, personality, persona, from the Latin: *persona*, actor's mask, character).

We seem to automatically shift gears whenever we are in diverse company, to somehow assimilate into the situation. This is not necessarily a problem when it's done for the sake of harmony; when one's principles and individuality are not compromised; when one is *aware* of the process. Problems arise when Mulengro is present and when a person unconsciously glamours themselves for the sake of pleasing another, to the detriment of one's true self. This so often happens in the mating game, when either a man or a woman seeks to draw their mark into intimacy. It occurs at corporate and political levels. It is the chameleon state assumed by those who are under threat; it happens in families all too often when a child is expected to conform to a required status quo.

A witch has done the work. A witch will recognize the game. A witch will take the mask on and off as is required . . . but a witch knows what the mask is!

I once wrote a story called *A Quest of Veils* that talks about all the identities we assume to enable us to feel worthwhile, and how difficult it becomes for others to read a person who doesn't pretend. When there is no game and nothing to win or lose, one holds a vital power. You see, a persona, a glamouring, is like a mirror, and the image in the mirror is something of whoever looks into its glass. Understand this; contemplate it.

You withdraw behind a veil, become occult, when there is no mask—people cannot recognize you because you do not reflect something of themselves back to them. You make no sense (as such you are almost mantled in the cloak of invisibility); no one can guess you. It's also the ultimate in psychic protection, but it won't endear you to many people because they cannot justify themselves to an unrecognizable property. It's a little like Aikido—it's all in the movement, so that even though you're *there*, you're able to be *elsewhere* with the least effort.

To know yourself intimately is the first key in the art of glamouring; to be able to read each situation is the second key; to know that glamouring is a mask that can be put on or taken off *at will* is the third key. Know that you are ordinary. Know that all of nature and all that is deemed supernatural is ordinary. Know that the cosmos, the universe, galaxies, ghosts, entities, change, life, and death are all ordinary. So that no matter how grand a thing appears, or how small, it is never other than comparative to you—ordinary. Ordinary presupposes common ground, but ordinary does *not* imply boring or unpredictable. *It simply excludes nothing!*

The very fabric of time, space, matter, and energy are as ordinary as you, are relative to you, *are* you. Therefore, they can be played with.

The sorcery of glamouring is dependent on the circumstances. Understanding that you are in touch with all things allows you to present whomever you choose to be into whatever circumstance. It is a garment, not a lie; it becomes a lie if you believe it to be who you are in order to deny who you are.

The art of glamouring is very well-known to those who desire success in the fields of advertising, politics, sales, self-development, corporate business, and theater. First, you need to emulate those you desire to attract or effect; secondly, you need to study and understand body language; thirdly, you need to understand the jargon of those you desire to attract or effect; and you need to research the field of those you desire to attract or effect; lastly, you need to acquire a personal and unique way of expressing yourself in relation to all of the above so that you are not an obvious interloper.

What is interesting is that doing all of the above tends to transform you into just what you are desiring, as that much observation and education over a lengthy duration would change a person to some degree. That's okay if you want to change your lifestyle overall; what would be terribly uncomfortable, though, is if you felt that you were really a liar, a charlatan—if the face that you present to those you seek to attract or effect has no substance to support the glamouring.

The witch also uses glamouring. Know what it means! A knowledge of all of the above is advantageous, especially when working with many people. It will allow others of diverse backgrounds to be very comfortable in your presence, especially when you are a healer, advisor, guardian, or teacher. Knowledge of glamouring will help you enter into psi-empathy and telepathic union with those you seek to attract or effect by educating not only your powers of observation, but also your energy field.

On an even more profound level, is a witch's understanding of this quote from my *Book of Shadows*:

### That which I adore I also invoke . . .

Seek to understand the archetypes, or faces, of your God and Goddess through a learned understanding of what they represent, through invocation of their powers, and through opening yourself to them in order to be a vessel for their influence within the realm of manifestation. This art of glamouring is done within the bounds of a ritual circle. It is the priest/priestess in communion, in conjunction with our aspirations expressed in one or many of the archetypes that our Lady and Lord are known to represent in nature. After many years of this manner of ritual, the residue of these invoked powers becomes deeply ingrained within each of us. *This* form of glamouring is energetic and is not dependent on external trappings to support it.

# REIVINGS, BANISHINGS, AND WARDS (INCLUDING SEALS AND SIGILS)

## Practicalities

There are lots of unwanted and random energies and entities floating around one's environment. The following techniques are required understandings for any witch. You will need to keep your own environment clear of these unwanted wraiths, and you may also, over time, be called on by others to clear these things from their houses or their lives.

Nothing ever goes away, you must understand. Things that are made of matter are not made *only* of matter, and can just as easily be energetic. Matter does not imply intelligence—soul does (and that's a rather ineffable concept). So why is it considered that intelligence inhabits only things of a material nature (like biological species)?

Entities can be either material or nonmaterial. They can be left over from extreme emotional discharges. They can be other and therefore, not of a recognizable origin.

My young years, inclusive of the practice of Witchcraft, were varied experientially for the sheer pleasure achieved from exploration and experimentation. I went from an involvement with the then-Psychic Research Society in Sydney (ghostbusting, for goodness sake!) to replying to calls from those who had heard of me (however), taking many of the coven members with me and checking out situations associated with things-that-go-bump-in-the-night. Many of these so-called phenomena were unsubstantiated, but a few were not, and only one of those was downright terrifying (a story I later told my kids when they were having slumber parties and creating "The Ghost Story" to freak each other out—my tale being all the scarier to them because it had actually happened). Many, even recently, were due to the unrealized power of Koori magic—the interference and disrespect of blind people into their sacred territories raising forces from the sleeping that should not have been disturbed. These powers are often earth elementals, and I work *only* at protecting the individuals who are affected by them. I *do not* attempt to disturb these powers further by my meddling in that which is none of my concern. There are Kadaicha in my area who need not be told by me or anyone else about these disturbances. They'll deal with whatever is required. I mention this because wherever you are, you need be aware of the ways of the sacred that are the ways of others, and seek to synchronize your undertakings accordingly.

One particular haunting in the bushy outskirts of Sydney, many years ago, was exactly this kind of situation. The people who had bought the land had a lot of money at their disposal, and were quite ignorant of occult matters. They had built this huge monstrosity of a house, put in both the indoor and the outdoor swimming pools (complete with statuary in the style of the ancient Greeks), and had, out of boredom on several consecutive evenings, played a game called Ouija, calling on whatever spirit could move the glass to answer their foolish questions. Phenomena began occurring, nightly, thereafter. A wall partition would shudder in pulsing waves, windows would refuse to open or close. The people would lock the house at night (including whatever windows that would close) to find the entire house wide open next morning—every morning! Their adult daughter, very pregnant at the time, began dreaming of horrifying mutilations to her unborn baby and was told, night after night, in her dreams, that she would not live through labor.

The mother of the household found me through the then-New Awareness Center in Chatswood, where I was conducting weekly workshops on occultism. I agreed to come to her home with several of my associates to check things out. We went equipped with our ritual tools and other materials we thought may be necessary to work a banishing, should there actually be something to banish.

The experience was astonishing. Three of us worked our way through the house, placing sensitive taping equipment in certain rooms that felt weird, while being increasingly aware of a piece of cold that was following us from room to room (of which there were many) seeming to be seeking to attract our attention. All this time the inhabitants of the house were confined to the kitchen.

Two coven members were, meanwhile, out scanning the grounds (about three acres of it, bordered by the Ku-ring-gai Forest) and one of the men spotted first one rock with distinct markings and symbols shallowly carved into its surface, then another and another and another. The whole area was marked with them!

They joined us inside with their news. We had, by this time, completed our feel of the house and had recovered the recording systems. There was nothing to be heard on the first one. On the second was the faint, but distinct, sounds of what seemed like two clacker sticks being rhythmically struck together, advancing on the sound system, then retreating.

We were sure that the séances the family had happily entered into as a game had awakened something from the earth of the place. The clear sensation that we all got, though, was that it didn't want to be awakened; that it wanted to be at one with the earth. It couldn't return on its own. It had to be sung back. We would have to suffice, as we knew of no Kadaicha at the time. So we sang it back the best we could.

We sat the family down in their lounge room when we had completed our rite and spoke to them of the sacred stones around the property (of which they were completely unaware). We warned them of the responsibility of living on consecrated ground, and that it seemed they had woken the thing that had been disturbing them. We suggested they leave the Ouija alone.

Some weeks later, an associate of mine contacted me about a supposed haunting that was occurring near the Ku-ring-gai Forest and asked if I wanted to come along to assist with the treatment. I asked for details, and it was the same family playing with the Ouija board. I refused to go.

Fairly recently, I was contacted by a local woman who lives in a secluded house not far from town. She had been beaten in a very violent domestic situation. Her life had been threatened at knifepoint by her lover, in front of her young daughter. She had called the police, charged him with assault, and had an apprehended violence order placed on him, effectively telling him to keep away from her. He didn't. She was sure it was him sneaking around her house in the deep night, night after night. She had heard something; her daughter had heard someone rustling outside. She came home one afternoon to find her bedroom swarming with maggots. No dead thing could be found. The house was securely locked. He'd had a key. She came to me to place protections around her property. I went with another initiate and did just that—with the desired effect.

# REIVING (CLEARING A PLACE)

To psychically clear unwanted entities is also called reiving (see Part Two, Section Two). Banishing often accompanies reiving, but reiving can also be performed to tranquilize a house or an environment that has been cluttered by previous occupants.

You will require a container of consecrated water, your athame, incense, and censer, a candle for each room, and a vacuum cleaner. It's often preferable to work with another person, but not strictly necessary. You are better to get rid of any occupants of the property. You are to work privately whenever possible. The energies of cowans can be unpredictable.

Every psychic knows that accumulated psychic grunge is heavier than air and will fall to the floor (and sometimes stick to windows). So the first thing that I do is vacuum the floors *with intent*. A vacuum cleaner is one's contemporary besom (broomstick), and much quicker than the manual tool; I do this myself. There's no point having the house occupants do it, it just never feels as clean. I will then set up a candle in each room, light it, and close off whatever doors there are. I get the charcoal burning, then take a shower with intent of purification.

Each room, from one end of the house to the other, is to be lightly encircled with your dagger (these encirclements are meant to be embracing rather than encapsulating), encircled with the smoke of the incense, and encircled with the consecrated water. With each circumambulation, you will raise aloft each implement to the four directions, calling on their powers of protection and harmony. As you exit each room, you will extinguish the candle with your fingers (don't blow it out), and leave the door open.

When you are done, you are to pack up all your things and leave without entering into conversation with anyone.

## BANISHING (GETTING RID OF A THING)

The occupants of the place you are to banish are to understand *beforehand* that they are not to engage in any form of dispute in the place, or to sully it with resentful or bitter emotions for the cycle of one Moon after your work. More often than not, their behavior would have been empathetic with whatever entity was causing them discomfort. Things are attracted to strong blasts of emotion as much as they are attracted to psychic activity. I like to call this the iron-filings-to-a-magnet syndrome, and you need to be aware of this phenomenon in association with all your magical practices, but especially where protections and enchantments are concerned.

Your banishing is irrespective. It matters not whether the entity is a living person or an energetic agent. Banishing is about getting rid of, but "getting rid of" requires full reiving of a property (see Reiving, this Section) and encirclement of its boundaries, as well as the correct placing of pentagramic seals.

You must attend to two priorities before you go *near* the place! First, you will seal off all orifices, psychic and actual, of your own body. A man has twelve, a woman has thirteen. For both: eyes, nostrils, ears, mouth, nipples, umbilicus, anus (eleven). For a man: penis (twelve). For a woman: vagina and urethra (thirteen). Secondly, you will take with you your boline, just in case you encounter the need for self-defense.

You will work the same process as reiving, but you will seal each portal of the house with a banishing pentagram of Earth. You will keep the intent of banishing clearly in focus at all times (words or no words).

You will work from a central point in the house to the outermost part of the property. You will conclude by encircling the entire property and laying seals on the ground at all entrances and exits.

# WARDING (KEEPING A THING OUT)

Warding is keeping out unwanted influences.

This is trickier than the previous two techniques because you'll require certain powers to assist you. You would not do *any* of these techniques as a beginner, anyway, so you'll have had plenty of time to accumulate the requirements of warding. They are certain talismans that you'll have gathered from the wild places, like bird skulls, feathers, bones, spiders' webs, the discarded bits of animals that have moved from whatever form they inhabited before they died to that form, certain stone entities and wood entities, specific shells, and symbolic amulets. All of these kinds of things will call you, and you will collect them. They will be part of your company of entities and are like familiars but are not the same, for their powers are dormant until they are formed as wards.

You will also need to acquire sealing wax.

Before a warding, prepare as you would for a banishing. You will also need to choose whichever of your company of entities you require to create the ward.

*A ward is an intelligent, elemental entity* (and could be considered a witch's medicine bundle with a specific purpose). A ward is always to come back to you (it is to be left to do its work for a limited cycle only (e.g., one lunar month, more or less). You are to tell no one of what you are doing, as the ward, once it is placed, is to remain undisturbed.

You are to bless and consecrate all things that make up the ward (you won't need much; keep it simple), wrap it in cloth or leather, and seal the way into the package with sealing wax. The ward will remain active until you break the seal yourself.

You will also require a small piece of meat. This will be buried on the property and the ward will remain active while the meat decomposes. It will feed the ward.

You are to ascertain that your scent is on both the package and the meat, so rub them both with your hands before you leave them at the site.

You will create the ward beforehand in your own home, within a cast circle. On the night of the warding, cleanse with intent of purification and seal your orifices with consecrated water. Take your athame and a bottle of consecrated water, as well as a packet of ordinary table salt. You will also require a small hand trowel (or a bloody shovel if the ground is presumed hard!).

You will go once around the property or the area casting a circle of protection. You will repeat the encircling with the consecrated water, and go around a third time sprinkling a fine circle of salt.

All is to be done with focus and intent. You are to be really clear about who you want to keep out!

You will summon the entity, that is, the accumulative of all things within the ward, to come out into the area of protection (these entities, once released, are never small, I warn you, but they *are lovely*; they are *your* creatures!). You will then bury the ward very well and very secretively, placing a rock over the spot if possible to dissuade any passing beastie from digging it up. You'll bury its food close by (ditto with another rock).

Then cut a zone into the circle with your athame allowing those in alliance with the person you are assisting to come and go, but you will seal it with a banishing pentagram of Earth.

Then you leave. You are to tell the person you are assisting that you have set up protections for a certain duration only, and that you will return to remove them when the allotted time is up. They are to understand this and to agree to do whatever they must, in that time sequence, to prevent further dysfunction.

At the appointed time, you are to return to the site and dig up your ward, summoning the entity back to you. You will then return home, break the seal, and put the bits back in their usual places, where they will remain dormant (which is their current, natural state).

Should the person you are assisting still be in danger after the allotted time, you are to fith-fath the aggressor if you still choose to remain involved.

## SIGILS AS SEALS

In this instance, we are talking about longterm talismans of protection that can be set wherever you choose. You will require however many flat stones you want. You will, within a cast circle, paint the predecided sigils on them, encircle them with the paint, and consecrate them by Earth, by Air, by Fire, and by Water, charge them with your athame, and will their purpose, through your dagger, into them. There are many books on specific seals and sigils pertinent to differing magical traditions, but these are patterns of your own deciding, specific to your intent.

Once created, they are to be left at the desired places for as long as protection is required.

# DREAMWALKER
## (INCLUDING ASTRAL PROJECTION)

There are doorways to many functions, and recognizing, retrospectively, what has been happening or where you have been, is important. Following are the different states of the realm of dreams.

- There's the voyage through your own mindscape: the sort function whereby bits and pieces will be remembered, seemingly disjointed, of your daily routine. It's like a cleanup function that sorts, categorizes, interfaces, and stores according to relevance and memorability the many experiences of apparent waking reality. These dreams are often seemingly scattered, irrational, but that's because the sort function doesn't depend on apparent logic or linear perspective. It just sorts the bits (like ants carrying necessary loads to the appropriate places in the nest).

- There are the dreams that relay information to your consciousness by way of symbolism (which is how the subconscious communicates, which is why imagery and emotion are the primary tools in spellcrafting) usually at times of profound change. The skill of translating the symbols into understandings has become a specific field of psychoanalysis, when it were better left in the hands of shamans and mystics who do not seek to categorize symbolic experience into neat and tidy interpretations that are cast as constants. Certain schools of psychotherapy view symbols like the snake in fixed, sexual terminologies, whereas this figure can have profoundly differing interpretations depending on who the dreamer is.

- Dreams of a symbolic nature are teachings from deep, personal experience for the purpose of transforming limited patterns or perspectives.

- You can have dreams that are precognitive, that prophesy events yet to occur within the waking timescape.

- It is possible to drop through one dream into a deeper dream, of memory or symbol, and to interact between both while knowing that you are dreaming, so as to be certain of recall.

## Astral Projection or Out-of-Body Dreams

- There are those powerful dreams whereby you leave the landscape of recognizable reality and voyage, through the dreamweb, to other worlds wherein you also live, retaining the memory of experiences upon waking into your current recognizable reality.

- There are dreams of waking whereby you have not awoken—parallel existence.

- Then there are the times when you'll meet with gods or beings from the landscape of magic; the times when you'll be in the company of people you know from the past, present, or future.

- Dreams of vehicles and modes of transportation are astral projections into symbolic transitional states. For example, train dreams are death dreams, and the dreamer usually encounters a station or terminal at which they embark. Most of the time, the dreamer is a watcher of the transition rather than a participant in it (participants are the dead). Airplanes, buses, cars, trucks, motorbikes, and boats are all differing modes of transition.

- Dreams of being a watcher are common for both me and many of my associates. Being insubstantial throughout, relaying messages to other people that were given to *you*, instead of *them*, so that the message would carry the desired impact (or would be detoured due to the other person dreaming elsewhere).

I did a Tarot reading in August of 1996 for a Sagittarian woman with whom I became good friends afterward (through mutual associates). She died in a light aircraft crash the following May. I tape all my readings, but in over twenty years of predictions, I have never retrieved the tape of someone who has died. I got this one back. In several instances, it mentions a death experience:

"Looks like there'll be a death in the family . . . no, it's you!"

At one stage, she asked, "Will I live in M—?"

I answer, "No, you'll be buried there."

At the beginning of the tape, I say, "Boy, have you got a health problem coming up! You'll be on fire and then, bang!, you're through it!"

The plane burst into flames on takeoff, just above the tree line. What was astonishing was that her experiences of living were to continue *after death*, as though nothing of impact had really happened. These are on tape. One of the experiences was of her going to Sydney "not for the reasons you think you're going," for lots of tests and examinations; another was of how angry she'd be at the authorities performing these tests and of how she'd be in the Department of Births, Deaths, and Marriages while she was there. Her body was flown to Sydney for an autopsy before the death certificate was validated, and the death recorded in that department, *but she would be there to experience these things, consciously.* There are several other postdeath experiences on the same tape.

Contemplation of all this raised a theory of parallel lives; as though we experience lives like outward-facing multifacets on a sphere—recognition of each being realized only at the center—one life being experienced multifariously. Another symbol of parallel lives being an infinitely mirrored kaleidoscope, the whole-self being the pieces that are not mirrored knowing themselves through their refraction.

## ASTRAL PROJECTION (O.B.E.—OUT-OF-BODY EXPERIENCE)

There is a difference between astral projection and astral traveling, or out-of-body experience. Astral travel occurs while in the sleep state (see Dreamwalker this Section) and during close-to-death encounters. You have probably heard of cases where, at the time of clinical death, or in operating rooms, the astral body has taken over the greater part of consciousness. This occurrence is due to the center presuming the onset of body-death. It has also been documented as occurring at times of emotional crisis or when an individual is under enormously distressing conditions.

As biological creatures, we have powerful life-sustaining instincts that engender strong defense responses to threats to the status quo, and the subconscious mind will seek to prevent any experience endangering recognizable self-perpetuation. The subconscious mind is, however, allied to the center, which in turn responds to factors, depending on the soul's development, derived from various other planes of existence and their interaction with your lifescape. Often, to avoid overloading the foreground of one's consciousness, messages or understandings pass from these other planes, through the center, and are relayed only as far as the subconscious mind, which then directs the astral body to travel during the little death known as sleep (or to pass on the relevant information in symbol).

Astral projection is a conscious projection of oneself, as an entity. It is similar to thought projection, but in this technique you will be creating a *double* of your physical form and projecting it into an ethereal image of your choosing (quite often using one's own physical appearance).

# TECHNIQUES

## Phase 1

Night is the time to practice this technique, as you will require deep, undisturbed concentration, and the airways are less likely to be cluttered during the dark of the day. You will be using the visualization function initially, but instead of retaining internalization, you are going to externalize your consciousness (as in shapeshifting).

Seat yourself in your usual working position. Go into meditation to center yourself.

Visualize yourself standing directly in front of where you are.

Observe the back of your head, your height, your stance—everything about yourself that you can see. It is not possible to observe your own face in this context, just as it is not possible to observe your own physical form (except in a mirror), as we are aware only of our internalized externalization of image and not the way we appear to an observer.

Next you are to project your consciousness into your body. By this I mean that you are no longer the person observing, but the person being observed. Look around your immediate environment. Go to the doorway and walk around the room, looking at everything: look behind objects, inside cupboards and boxes, look closely at books, pictures, everything. Continue this exercise nightly until you are familiar with your immediate surroundings. Always reenter your prone material body the way you left.

## Phase 2

Begin with meditation. Go with the process of projecting into the externalized image of yourself. You may now proceed to leave the room with which you have oriented yourself over the preceding nights and travel around the house in which you live, observing at all times and remaining aware of all things your senses perceive. If there are other people in the house, you may pick up on their emotions, moods, dream patterns, etc., but at this stage, do not work at having them become aware of your presence (they may become aware of you anyway, especially if they are asleep and traveling close to their physical habitat). Continue with this exercise until you are familiar with the process.

## Phase 3

Begin with meditation. Project your consciousness into your self-image. You can now leave the house and move around outside. Be aware of the time. Observe all that is around you. Now you can begin the process of expanding your entity. If you bend your knees and jump, you will discover that you are weightless and can keep rising into the atmosphere as long as you desire. You can also *think* your astral body from one place to another without necessarily following a familiar route.

Practice this often, but don't forget to follow the return-to-body procedure! I tend to stress this like a mother-hen. I've had horrible postastral dysfunction occur due to both interruption and lack of experience, and it has sometimes been *days* before I stopped feeling dizzy and/or nauseous and disoriented. Sleeping lots tends to fix it, though.

## Phase 4

Begin as usual to the point of consciousness projection. Previously arrange with a close associate to project to their house at a certain time. Anything observed by your associate is to be recorded by them, and you are to record all that you have observed immediately upon return to your material body.

## Phase 5

Do as ye will . . .

- If you are blocked from projecting anywhere, there is always a particular reason. You can leave it alone or explore why, but be careful.

- Manipulating the consciousness of others while in this state is unethical.

- Communicating to a sleeper while in an astral state can have disastrous consequences if you have underlying emotional issues, as these issues will be what the sleeper hears—subconscious to subconscious—be aware of your own motives!

# OMENS AND PORTENTS
## (INCLUDING MORE ABOUT THE GEAS)

Again, we enter into a prospective danger zone. Not (never!) due to the subject matter, but due to the consistent misuse of techniques by certain members of occult communities by way of overkill.

Remember, earlier in this text, when I discussed the good witch as being someone who was proficient, as opposed to one who is on the way to becoming so? This applies here. A good witch, in all matters, will consider her own opinions, relative to circumstances, as either correct (in the interpretation of current data) or in training to become so; honoring the opinions of another, when that other is more adept, is sacrosanct.

Circumspection is a requirement for any adept in any field.

I become heavy-handed in my discussion of this subject because for almost thirty years I have mingled with occultists, either of my own lineage or others, and so very often I have seen others pull out Tarot, consult runestones, and peruse ephemeredes for the most inconsequential drama or desire. *This dilutes the powers of psychic aptitude.* You must not become reliant on any outside thing to the detriment of your own power or you will lose the capacity to create! And you will become diminished.

Awake! Be aware of what passes you, of what touches you, of the color of the day. Listen to the pattern of your lifescape and recognize whatever speaks to you that usually doesn't. Carpe diem!

The techniques of Tarot, astrology, runes, I Ching, etc., are oracular and/or prophetic, and are, therefore, a different subject altogether. To consult them haphazardly is dangerous to the state of one's mental health; it can confuse the senses and can become quite addictive.

The reading (or recognition) of omens and portents depends on your geas, so first we'll deoccultate what that is: a geas is somewhat like an unremovable curse. It is akin to destiny, but is not destiny. It pushes you or pulls you. It's the reason you are witch and not something else. It's the reason you will sometimes feel a sense of urgency, foreboding, or excitement when there is seemingly nothing to warrant those feelings. A geas is your own personal haunting *by yourself!* You *know* you can't escape it. It sometimes feels like a responsibility. Kassandra, a Greek prophetess who always envisioned dreadful happenings, had a geas on her. She might have wanted to be a queen or a housewife, a warrior or a merchant, but she wasn't (even though a geas won't interfere in any of your pursuits). She became legendary for the geas that propelled her to prophesy dreadful happenings.

Being a reputable psychic could be considered, by others, a gift or a curse—to the psychic, it's their geas. It's what they do that's akin to the body they inhabit—it *just is!*

Learning to dance with one's geas is essential to one's mental health. I developed a kind of sideways skepticism toward what is termed phenomena (of a psychic/occult nature) at a young age. I was prone then to the seeking of sensationalist manifestations of power, as were most of my colleagues (and at seventeen that was everybody!), to the degree that now, in my forties, I can accurately predict an intimately detailed future crisis through the Tarot as easily as I can plan my evening meal. I realized long ago that I can't let any of it get to me, but there's so much more to it than I'm prepared to go into. You will need to function, albeit passionately, on a day-to-day level, and therefore it is appropriate that you recognize and register an omen (in the discordant or frenetic call of birds, for example) and go on alert rather than altering your plans in any dysfunctional way. If the omen is big enough to warrant running for shelter, then by all means don't ignore it!

An omen or a portent is like a link to a forthcoming event. Your connection to all things (and all times, past, present, and future) means that you know, at some level or another, all that is occurring everywhere, in all time zones. What is *relative* to you can be recognized *by* you, through a medium that is *not* you, and this is called an omen, or a portent.

## Examples

- An adrenaline attack out of the blue, for no obvious reason, that is twenty minutes in duration, is a field of something or someone passing you by. Take note of it, but do not go looking in your own head to find out what's wrong—just do a quick, but definite, scan of your life to ascertain whether there is anything unresolved or dysfunctional. If there's not, then it is someone (or something) else's trouble.

- A total stranger comes up to you in the street and says one or two distinct sentences to you and continues on. When you look to see where they are going and they're gone, take note of what was said. Chances are they are not from our recognizable reality.

- A sequence invades your day: the same, or similar, things are said by seemingly random people. Your awareness of the pattern of the sequence puts you on alert.

- You see fleetingly someone you know, again and again, only to realize it's someone else. You will either be contacted by that person or you must make contact.

- You dream of someone you know well. Tell them what you have dreamed. The message will be important to them either now or soon.

- Uncommon cloud formations, changes in the atmosphere, unusual things with birds, ants, spiders, cows are easy ones—all portend weather changes.

- Glimpsing an animal or bird in intimate or rare expressions of interaction are *gifting* omens that portend joyous experiences or powerful realizations.

- Waking deep within the night without apparent reason. Something will have called to you. Open yourself to contemplation.

- The overwhelming desire to encircle yourself or your environment—do it!

- The overwhelming desire to get away from whomever you are with; to be alone to work ceremony—do it!

It's all geas. Omens and portents are looping tools that the geas will use automatically to enable it to fulfill your destiny. It's all natural. It's as natural as the function of your heart beating!

## *Tarot*

Ominous . . .
This built-up haze of rage upon a people!
Weave softly through it . . .
They do not know I taste them when they're lying;
On the surface they pretend, inside they're dying . . .
And all the while they say how hard they're trying
But trying doesn't work—to live you do it!

They fear me for I tell them what they're hiding
Deep beneath the well-kept faces of the young;
I tell them every buried song unsung;
Every sight and every slander of the tongue;
Of the hell into which slowly they are sliding.

I am Tarot; Revolution;

I'm the Raven that sits, and whispers, on your shoulder . . .
I can name the savage beast that lurks behind you;
I'm the mirror of the Thing you hope won't find you
And you fear me, for I cannot but remind you
That you're older now . . . and will get so much older.

She comes to see herself in my reflection
In the hope that I will tell her nothing's wrong;
That behind the weak betrayal she is strong . . .
That she can change the places where she can't belong . . .
That she can handle life without love's lost affection.

How I want to set them free!
See them treat life tenderly!
Have them know that they are me!

Malevolent . . .
The stealing hand of "How do I survive?"
That chokes him like the grief of Lilith's daughter;
That takes his breath away and makes him fear;

"Is there anybody" begs he softly, "who can hear?"
"Someone who won't make me 'goat-to-slaughter'?
"Because I'm drowning but I cannot see the water!"

> I beg them "Dance!!"
> I cry "Alive!!"
> I scream out "Live it more; don't merely just survive!
> You have the Name of it within!
> To waste life *is* the only sin . . .
> To taste the holy bloody feast of life's creation
> Is your *first* and *last* and *only* obligation!"

I am the song of you that calls you to awaken;
The archer and the bow, not just the arrow!
She speaks for me; but I am you, forsaken!
I *am* you, always was, down to the marrow;
The deep and ancient future . . .
I am Tarot!

—from *The Feast of Flesh & Spirit* by Ly de Angeles

# THE ART OF INVISIBILITY

The crafting necessary for invisibility is dependent on who, or what, you want to hide. A couple of these techniques are as much common sense as they are magic, but I'm sitting here at my keyboard and many instances of requests for invisibility are passing through my thoughts, and due to the nature of some of those requests, I am loathe to speak. You will understand my motives when you have been asked for the spell. I do not want to lead anyone into the exceedingly gray areas that require confidentiality on the part of the working witch.

What *is* certain is that invisibility can be a tool for protecting certain people for a specific time duration. Time-duration invisibility is required when you take over the responsibility of another's destiny while they complete some task or other wherein there lies a risk (should they be noticed). I have done these heavy-duty enchantments of invisibility only a few times in my life, and always for as short a time as is possible. Otherwise, rebound is a very real prospect.

You can work this technique using a fith-fath of the person, but it is not nearly as effective as having them with you in the flesh. You are going to temporarily banish the person, you see, and without a distinct, short-term time frame, not only could the individual you have banished cease to be (like die!), but they could, also, simply disappear, which would leave you stuck with the consequences of the *ghost of the reason for the invisibility spell* attaching itself to your destiny! The person who has made the request for the spell of invisibility *must* agree to your terms and promise to return to you for the removal of the shade when the allocated time frame is complete!

So . . . the technique is quite simple. You will require your cloak, four dark blue, gray, or black candles, your white cord, incense and censer, a lighter, and your athame. It is best to

work this enchantment on the wane of the Moon, but sometimes necessity requires spontaneity.

# THE RITE

## Part 1

1. Wrap the person in your cloak and seat them on the floor in
   the center of the environment prepared for the rite. Coil
   your cord around them closely, forming a tight circle. Place
   the four dark candles at the compass points just outside this
   little circle.

2. Cast a circle around you *and* the inner circle. Light the
   four dark candles and the incense (the incense is, necessarily for this spell, very smoky, so you will require lots of oil
   in the mix).

3. Encircle the cloaked figure seven times, widdershins (counterclockwise in the Northern Hemisphere, clockwise in the
   Southern Hemisphere), visualizing deeper and deeper mist
   forming around them with each step. Facing the little circle
   from the gate of Earth, banish the person, by the power of
   Earth, by describing the banishing pentagram of Earth with
   your athame. You will do likewise for Air, Fire, and Water.

4. When this is done, take the incense and walk around the person in the opposite direction (deosil), seven times. You will
   then open your own circle with your athame and ground the
   energy as you have been taught. *Blow out* the candles—Earth,
   Air, Fire, and Water—and undo the little cord circle, *coiling
   the cord as you do so* (you will not uncoil the cord until the
   time frame is complete and when you re-encircle the person

to undo the enchantment). Remove the cloak and put it away. Tell the person not to speak to you again until they return. Tell them to dress as inconspicuously as possible during the time frame, to be as normal as usual, and to discourage eye contact with others as much as possible. Then tell them to leave.

Keep the four dark candles for the rite of completion, but have four red candles ready for that night.

## Part 2

1. When the time frame is over and the person comes back to you, you will repeat Part 1 up to where you originally encircled them seven times (*you won't do that this time*).

2. Describe an *invoking* pentagram of Earth at the Earth gate, directed *inward* toward the cloaked figure in the center of your circle, then Air, Fire, and Water. When this is done, you are to uncoil the cord and leave it loose on the floor. Then remove the cloak.

3. Light a red candle from the dark candle at Earth, snuff out the dark candle, remove it from the holder, and replace it with the red candle. Do the same for Air, Fire, and Water. Have the person step out of the ring of candles and stand, waiting, while you disengage your own outer circle and earth the power. Only then will you snuff the red candles.

4. Tell the person:

**You're back. You will stay back.**
**I will not do this for you again.**
**Take these candles and get rid of them.**
(hand them the dark candles)
**Don't keep them and don't leave them available**
**for anyone else to burn!**
**Go in peace,**
**but you must phone me within twenty-four hours**
**just to have a quick, casual conversation.**

The phone call is to fully earth the rite. It must be done.

When the person leaves, take a shower with intent of reiving the field of the enchantment from your own field.

Other forms of invisibility are lighter:

- Banish a No Parking sign with the flick of a banishing pentagram.

- Visualize your energy field as misty and insubstantial when you are having a bad-hair day and don't want anyone to register your existence.

- When too many people want a piece of you, banish the telephone for a few hours or take your cloak and pass it around your body three times while expressing your desire for invisibility in a whisper with each pass of the cloak.

Know that you can't be seen. Don't be silly (like some witches I have known, myself included when I was young and vague) and cast a spell of invisibility about yourself and then go out on the town to see who can see you! That's like an oxymoron!

# PSI-EMPATHY AND PSYCHIC PROTECTION

By now, understanding the preceding work and putting it into practice, you will have become very finely tuned. This is not without its seeming drawbacks. I find it very difficult to be around large groups of people, as I pick up on the randomness and the chaos of desire and expectation that permeates these gatherings when the majority of people present do not know each other. They may be out for a good time (rallies for clear purpose of ideal do not exemplify this as most minds tend to be directed toward a goal or message), or may simply be part of a crowd in a plaza or on any big-city street. I become increasingly distressed, as psi-empathy cannot but hear the messages of energy and instinct that fill the airways.

Psi-empathy is very much telepathy. Psi-empaths are psychics of a particular caliber insofar as we need to establish clear boundaries around our own identities to prevent ourselves from merging with others (at the risk of losing one's distinct individuality). All witches who I train, and who have worked at the techniques inherent in that training, end up psi-empathic. You will find that you can be listening to someone talking and you can hear the words they're speaking, but you will also be hearing what they are saying *beneath, behind,* and sometimes, *as well as,* the surface topic. This, again, is often uncomfortable because it always occurs when there is a hidden, or denied, agenda, and what are you going to do? Tell them what you *really* hear? Tell them that they are lying? How much trouble you can afford to get yourself into must be taken into consideration. Chess! Consider chess (the art of strategy) when considering how to respond. Often, the expedient action is to get up and walk away from the conversation because, also often, the person with the hidden or denied agenda isn't going to like being exposed. What I refuse to do is to pretend to accept whatever lie is coming out of their mouth or whatever they are out to prove by their covert communication.

The first step in psychic protection is to purposely avoid these kinds of people. Look to your own motives for engaging in their company. The second step is to heed your own instinct. The third step is to respond, determined by your appraisal of the situation, with the appropriate action.

# VAMPIRISM

I run the risk of sounding slightly paranoid when I tell you there is *a lot of this*, but I'm being extremely real and very serious.

Let's throw away the Count Vladimir the Impaler image. Let's relegate to someone else's lifescape the concept of the go-for-the-throat night stalker, and let's talk about the wannabes. These are your Western-style vampires and they dwell in the shadows of other people's lifescapes, sucking on their lifeforce to substantiate their existence and wearing the masks of niceness to perpetuate their own lack. They are usually very adept at vampirism, learning from a young age how to get what they want without effort or conscience, having been taught how to "suck" by other vampires. They're difficult to identify, initially, wearing the guise of *kind* to attract your attention, and attentive they will be—buying their way into your lifescape by way of flattery or gifts (remember not to eat or drink while dwelling in the land of faerie!). They will talk the jargon of your language, but they will seek to have you tell them of their importance, their potential, their prowess. They will seek to, in some way, become you!

One of my dearest initiates in Victoria, Glynys, set herself up as my minder for a while, as I had been recently published for the first time and was naïve to the wiles of those who came, usually uninvited, to seek my company. Glynys was the finance manager of a large banking corporation at the time and she worked out a mean, an average, over several weeks, of the number of people passing through my home in a day. That average was thirty-five people. Glynys coined the phrase "Ly clones." These were wannabe witches, keeping company with witches, talking about the Craft, dressing the part, and drinking from those who *are* witches—until they are recognized.

How do you recognize one? Gifts and flattery—just to be able to talk solely about themselves. Gifts and flattery—seeking to buy their way into a field that requires doing. The moment they are confronted as to their motives, they become excessively offended and you probably won't see them again. Gifts and flattery are all very nice, but always ascertain what the giver wants in return.

Vampirism feels terrible. You will be sitting in the company of a vampire and you'll begin to feel a belly pull, a head squeeze, fatigue, anxiety, and even nausea. They do not entertain clean conversation, and when you attempt to really discuss a subject of interest, they will always pull the conversation back to themselves. They invariably talk *at* you and not *with* you.

If you have fallen into the trap of being around a vampire for any length of time (and Mulengro is always their game), remember that it is very easy to be caught by one. They are rampant. You *must* cleanse yourself of their energy by showering, swimming, or bathing with intent (reiving). They can leave a kind of *clag* (residue) attached to your energy field, as they have been puncturing your field, sucking or biting bits from it, while in your company.

Psi-empathy is a clear tool, as opposed to rationale or manners, for living the magic without disruption. Experience is not disruptive. Experience is experience. It's the *other* teacher (other than your own guidance). Psi-empathy is the range of extension of your energy field, including the tendrils you sends out on telepathic journeys, and your awareness of what is touching this field is paramount for your protection.

We will not spend much time on psychic attacks as, you are to understand, only a very adept occultist or an extreme emotional cripple can achieve this feat. You would have had to have let them in for them to have breached your personal boundaries (Sun Tzu's *Art of War* discusses what to do if you've let the enemy inside your defenses—in love and war, gifts and flattery). Many people claim psychic attack when it is not so. Simply because one's life is in seeming disarray does not mean one is under attack; it's likely one has left things undone, unresolved, and this must be attended to in order for disarray to transform into art.

## GHOSTS AND HAUNTINGS

The ghosts and hauntings covered in this section are not the ectoplasmic kind, but the memory, or the transference, kind. Be clear not to take on another's ways (like your mother's, father's, boss's, or hero's), as you are *not* them. The attitudes of others who impress you (i.e., make an impression in whatever capacity) can be like ghosts—they can haunt your mind and possess you with their alien attitudes. All arguments are hauntings, as opposed to healthy debate or discussion. I'll leave you to contemplate this without filling in the examples.

Emotional cripples suffer from ghosts in the psyche and hauntings from the past, impeding their capacity to allow. Many emotional cripples can develop other powers to make up for their inability to function in equilibrium (if you can help or heal them without becoming subject to the transference of cause and effect, then by all means do so, but be careful, as many can drop off some unseen edge without forewarning). One of these powers is a subterranean psychic wildfire that can strike you, astrally, and leave you waking in terror or, conversely, unable to sleep due to unspecific anxiety.

Much in the way of psychic attack takes place when you are asleep and therefore vulnerable. If this happens, you are to encircle your bed, dome a pentagram of Earth-banishing over you, and *only then*, send out tendrils to seek the source of the attack. The source may be a random event sending out a harmonic that passes you in the night, but if you discover that the attack has a sinister source, you can deal with it through warding (or, as is warranted, fith-fathing).

Another (albeit temporary) form of psychic protection is to imagine the boundary of your energy field surrounded with outwardly directed mirrors, therefore reflecting the attack back on to your enemy.

## GETTING AND HEXING (THE HOWS, WHYS, PROS, AND CONS)

This is spellcrafting. You will employ whatever works for you. There are many fine books available that refer the practitioner to different and various techniques that either work or do not, depending on the technique/practitioner synergy.

(Hey! I'm sitting here typing, and a pencil, lying across from me, just bounced off the desk and hit the side of my head! Don't you just love it when weird things like that happen?!)

Okay. I can tell you the kind of spellcrafting that works for me. I'm not going to generalize or summon up other practitioner's techniques for your experimentation. You can explore for yourselves.

Most of Part Three has been guiding you to this point, and certain discussions in Part Two under the subject of the Four

Worlds (Relevant Notes on Qabbalah), so you will need to go back and forth to glean the entirety of the pattern to ascertain how the whole lot weaves together.

Spells of getting and hexing are always worked in a circle. You will focus your intent on the outcome and not the process, as it is necessary that you get out of the way of the process. This takes more practice than it sounds. To achieve an outcome *that is not necessarily inevitable to your destiny* (by your current assessment of events), patterns of flow will be diverted from their current course. This can precipitate any number of seemingly discordant extremes of experience. What is sure is that change requires change, and you must be willing to go with the flow of those changes, in perfect trust, realizing that they are the necessary process involved in the attainment of a specific outcome.

You are to know how you want to *feel* in response to the achievement of that outcome. The bricks and mortar of reason will get you into deep water here because you can achieve the realization of a goal only to find that it doesn't fit you. You could end up being very successful in the wrong place, in the wrong enterprise, with the wrong lover, or in the wrong job. What does "wrong" mean in this instance? It means that where you end up, or what you end up doing, is what you *thought* would make you happy because you didn't understand that it was *how you wanted to feel* that mattered—the bricks and mortar are irrelevant.

Once the feeling of the outcome is firmly understood, you will *sing* the event into manifestation, within your ritual circle, using a tool of focus (from the plaiting of threads to zoning out on a candle flame). The aim is to call the eventuality to you.

Gather, with focus and intent, as many bits and pieces as symbolize your desire. Be careful to cover all options. I once summoned a house in which to live considering clear specifications based on a burning desire for a particular feel in my living environment. I even specified that it was to have a fireplace as I don't like to be cold. I attained what I wanted, except I had neglected to specify a fireplace *that works*. The chimney had been removed and the roof had been tinned over. With that quirky little exception, the house is excellent for my tastes. So, specifics in the gathering of symbols is a requirement.

You don't want a lot of bulk to the spell (we're employing sympathetic magic here), and you want all things to be *willing* to symbolize your intent so that there will be a certain symmetry and interactive passion between the objects and the intent (that's a kind of creation). For example, possible ingredients for a love spell: red rose petals, white silk, jasmine oil, the idea of the person you desire written on vellum in a flowing script, leaves or twigs from an evergreen, a small piece of good bread to symbolize stability and nourishment, bells and shells to represent laughter and shelter, small gemstones of garnet and pearl— all placed in a black velvet pouch tied thrice with red thread.

You will consecrate your spell by Earth, by Air, by Fire, and by Water. You will sing it into life. You will bless it by sprinkling it with consecrated wine, and after you have completed the ritual, you will bury it in some fecund place and plant above it.

Similar things can be done to acquire money, position, dwellings, work, etc. You will simply need to consider what colors, textures, scents, and sensations are relevant to your spell, and seek to have them come together as a symphonious whole.

## Hexing

Hexing is *always* personal (as opposed to fith-fathing, which can be done to aid or fix the problems of another person). Hexing is slightly more difficult, as you will require things belonging to, or personal to, the person. Hexing is specific, whereas getting is preferably not. The bundle principle is the same; however, the ingredients will be more malefic than in spells of getting (e.g., other than the bits belonging to the person you want to hex, you will require such things as bent and rusty nails or pins; junk plastic; something that smells bad; your desire written in a stilting, jagged hand; and your anger tied once, twice, three times onto string. Place the ingredients into a paper bag (so that it breaks down quickly), tie it with string, and bury it.

If you have an unjustifiable reason for the sending of a hex, it will come back to you *with a vengeance.* Some say threefold; some say sevenfold; some say tenfold!

Hexing, however, need not always be nasty. It can be used to shut up a gossip or a slanderer; it can be used to curtail a devious business person from unjust or unscrupulous practices; it can be used to move a charlatan from your area; it can be used to curtail the behavior of a bully; it can be used to summon justice on someone who has gotten away from rightful prosecution on some technicality or other.

The pouch of magic is buried as in the getting spell, again, with an appropriate herb planted atop the site. Use lots of manure!

"Do as ye will, e'er it harm none" (go back and reread To Be Witch) is appropriate where both getting and hexing are concerned.

Two things to remember (at the risk of repeating myself): (1) don't meddle in other people's business, and (2) never boast, never threaten, just do, and do quietly.

# THE CIRCLES OF LIGHT AND DARK

Consider for a moment what life could be like for both yourself and the Earth on which we dwell if you could see and understand the patterns of change, in their cyclic entirety, without getting caught up in concepts of time and personalization. I recommend reflection on the circular rather than the linear. Consider that all things within the known universe revolve around each other in everwidening patterns, eternally and infinitely, from the smallest to the vastest, to the furthest reaches of revolution.

I once presented the following riddle to my students, "When does zero become one?" They went away for a week and on returning gave me a virtual deluge of esoteric answers. You will be given the answer, of necessity, because you cannot go away for a week and come back after consideration of this most simple riddle—one through which your thoughts will learn new clarity, one that requires answering in truth, as there can only be one answer—never! Zero is going to remain zero forever. One is going to remain one forever. They can only and forever relate to each other; they can never *be* each other. If you contemplate this, you will come to understand that *all* numbers (and they are considered sacred for good reasons, but that's another story) are possible when considering zero, and as such, zero remains infinitely pregnant with possibility. There is no such thing as nothing— the greatest and the smallest are merely relative to each other, and, therefore, reflect each other always.

Light and dark are to be considered in the same context. Light could be considered infinite in its possibilities, as could darkness. One can see light only in relativity to darkness. The positive, attractive, and expansive force of not only your own soul, but also of the universe, can be truly understood only if one takes the time to consider the negative, repulsive, and contracting—or the circles of light and dark.

I want to make it quite clear that the language of magic, and its ability to evoke reaction within the world, as it does between the worlds, is that of both image and symbol. When a concept is embodied in either an image or a symbol, it takes on a form of life that is not synonymous with the spoken or written word unless it *becomes* the word (i.e., a sigil of the enchantment that is summoned to represent what the spoken word could never do, despite the incredible power of the spoken and/or the written word when they are expressed in particular ways). This theoretical, practical manual is intended to summon from within you the images that represent more than the work. The spoken ritual, for example, without the attending visualizations, would be a gesture only, and would have no validity as a magical procedure (understand that the landscape of magic is between the worlds. You may work sorcery and ritual in the place of Assiah, your Earthplane temple, but it will reverberate through other planes of reality in order to effect your desire).

So, when working all magics of an external nature (i.e., those that affect your personal world, those that assist you with conscious, inspirational and creative pursuits, and the achievement of that to which you aspire), the circle of light is when and where you will work: the waxing lunar cycle (from New Moon to Full); the waxing solar year, for long-range projects (from Winter Solstice to the day prior to the Summer Solstice). When working with planetary influences, you will work when the planets concerned are direct, not retrograde, and when planetary or stellar influences are at zenith, not nadir.

When working all spellcrafting and ritual of an internal, repulsive (in the literal sense), or deep-diving nature, all banishings and bindings, you will work best when accessing the circle of dark: the waning lunar cycle (from the second day of the Full Moon to the day prior to the New Moon); the waning solar year, for long-range projects, from the Summer Solstice to the day prior to the Winter Solstice; when the planets or stellar influences are at nadir (retrograde is not advisable at all).

The work and the research that you perpetuate will prove invaluable, progressively, and self-alchemy will allow you to remain within your own disciplined, and well-charted limitations. These limitations, like Saturn, are merely there as guidance to personal control. To walk outside your own boundaries without first having acknowledged them means to lose control, and that will never do! This does not mean that you cannot explore the fullest potential of your emotional, physical, mental, or creative faculties; it means that within that fullness you do no harm. If, however, you do not realize your own limits, then you cannot supersede them, if that is what is required, or, like the Devil card, you run the risk of becoming trapped by them, therefore creating webs of unwanted habits, patterns, or obsessions.

The initiate cannot afford not to work at Saturn's gate!

The circles of light and dark are the spiral dance of cause and effect, ebb and flow, life and death, letting go and holding on, same and change, Goddess and God, and God and Goddess—be familiar!

## TRAINING—A YEAR AND A DAY THRICE OVER

Your initiation will begin a three-year process (it doesn't stop after that, but it is set and sealed). In traditional covens, you will undergo three degrees, or rites, of progressive initiation in those three years; but with or without these traditional marks of progression, as multi-experience has taught, these three phases *will* be realized within that cycle of three years, and there is pause for thought required in this understanding.

These three phases are known as First Rite (or Degree), Second Rite (or Degree), and Third Rite (or Degree). The Second and Third Rites are termed "the Deepening." The Second Rite will strike around a year and a day after your initiation. I say "strike" because it is a *danger zone.* You will be challenged by the forces of your calling, in whatever area you have taken for granted, and the stage will always be set in the ordinary world, the challenges will always be associated with your ego and your hidden agendas, and it is always devastating to some degree.

Second Rite is the alchemical phase of your training whereby the dross, self-delusionment, apathy, and cowardice of your ego will confront very real adversity. Through action, intent, and true response to this adversity, the crud is burned off, revealing the gold, the folded and tempered steel, the bread of your clear understanding and self-honor.

The third year sees you through it. In traditional covens, Third Rite bestows the position of elder and/or high priesthood. This is *not* a hierarchical power trip (which has been known to happen, unfortunately, in some obscure covens), but a responsibility to be a clear vessel for the flow of justice and compassion, a willingness to take on the requirements of a teacher, and the capacity to be responsible for the initiation of other witches. You will do this by knowing what to look for and how to respond to the real, as well as the illusory, in the pattern of the applicant. When you are in the position of high priesthood, you should be willing to take on the responsibilities of a coven and of the correct training of each of its members.

Third Rite, as a magical progression, will be the culmination of three years of living the Way of witch. High Priesthood, however, can be bestowed *only* through the sword of another who has been given that title through an order of succession. On this point I refuse to argue.

# THE THREE DEGREES OF PRIESTHOOD

## First Degree Priesthood

The growth that is achieved through this degree is through acknowledgment of the Earth as supreme provider. This degree opens the initiate to the Earth energies that affect us. The rituals worked by a witch are Earth/Moon, Earth/Sun, Earth/Star (the cycles and the seasons). Coming to understand the Ways of witch are the work of the First Degree witch, and that work is the basis of this book.

In addition to the personal interaction you will undertake with the elemental forces and the beings in the places of the realms of accessibility, your contemplation of Goddess and God, your alignment with one or the other of their faces and with the practicalities of the disciplines, you will want to explore certain Earth-focused crafts or skills. Many initiates, after fully understanding the Deepenings, find that they are drawn, naturally, into arts such as healing, herbal lore, husbandry, ecology, and environmental guardianship. Many initiates choose to specialize in these arts even after the challenge of Second Rite. The symbol of the First Degree Initiate is the pentacle. The Primum Mobile of First Rite is the Green Line.

## Second Degree Priesthood

Those initiates who have come to fully understand their inter-connectedness to the Earth and the energies that support life here, in all its diversity, will proceed to learn of the mysteries through the legends and mythologies of their chosen path. They may choose to look at the psychological implication of archetypal analogy, the effects of magic in consciousness, etc.

They are the way-showers who choose to teach others in the various capacities already existing in standard occult practices. They work the rites of Earth, Moon, Sun, and Stars, and live magic through the line of the Merlyn or Morgan le-fae. They are the musicians, the poets, the talkers, the storytellers, the writers, and the artists who express to others by way of both art and science. They teach by example. They may find themselves within the framework of modern society, *in* the world but not *of* it, and may often be found in standard, contemporary occu-pations while living and working the Craft and creating their art as a lifestyle.

The stuff of the Second Degree is the thing, as they say, of what legends are made, even if that is seen only by the person's loved ones and closest allies, those who will be around when the challenges strike, when the forces of the Way of the quest see what the initiate is made of. As long as you keep the faith and remind yourself that what is happening is training you, you'll break through the barriers that are what I call "the Dragon's Egg." You'll find the way to freedom.

For many initiates, the functions of the arts associated with magic are their natural line-of-least-resistance, and they will spe-cialize in the associated fields. Their symbol is the staff. The Pri-mum Mobile of the Second Degree Initiate is the Red Line.

## Third Degree Priesthood

The witches who have come to know of the Earth as the Great Provider, who have come to understand and be at one with the rituals and rites of their inheritance and the myths and mysteries of their line, will come to the thresholds and remain between-the-worlds.

These are the initiates of the inner mysteries, who seek to invoke the very essence of their goddess/god *into themselves* for the specific purpose of influencing the course of the evolving whole through their honor of the evolving whole—honor being the foundation stone (the Lia Fal) of them all. They are the star seeds, their purpose being to keep the magic on *this* side of reality. They are alive! to serve the forces of revolution (which, in esoteric terms, has to do with the innate rightness of the overall patterns of change). They are the walkers of the inner planes, and their temples, while being earthed in our considered reality, have their parallels in the deep and ancient future past.

The Third Rite Priestess or Priest is a warrior in the way of magic; in the ways of the sacred; tried and tested and undaunted by the appearances of the world of men—champions of Goddess; sisters and brothers of God—face to face. They dare to be different, will move out of mainstream lifestyles, and will keep the gate open.

They are the teachers of the initiates who are in, and passing through, the Green Line and the Red Line, as well as the passers-on of reestablished links with the ancient past to those who have learned and sought to work the way of magic in the now.

Their symbol is the sword. The Primum Mobile of the Third Degree is the Black Line. They are dragon riders, one could say—ragged though they may appear to those who cannot see them. Robed, often, in a weird anonymity that allows those who are kind to apprehend them easily, but not others. They use the art of glamouring well!

All witches are grail seekers.

I conclude our work here with the understanding of the three degrees for two reasons:

1.  So that you will not fail when the "shit hits the fan" at Second Rite (because it's simply like the musician who goes from scales to Bach!).

2.  Because I am High Priestess of the Black Line, and it is my geas to miss nothing in this work; to let you know, without embellishment, the pitfalls you may encounter.

It is also my will to ask you to make contact with me as the need arises, through my publisher, so that our relationship, and the network you may require, can proceed. Those of you who take the self-initiation are truly of my coven—the Coven of Crystalglade. This book is the training of the initiates of this coven (with a few exceptions, you understand, which I am oath-bound to shut up about). You are simply of a different kind, linked to us by the audacity of individuality! (I've always been a rebel). Given the auspices of circumstance, I hope that we may perchance meet, perhaps by word, if not by deed, along the timeline of the future or in a walk through the dreamscape!

Be ye blessed; blessed be!

# *The Feast of Flesh and Spirit*

### I

It's me, you see? . . .
The gypsy-woman-born-of-no-one,
Who holds this priest, her friend,
With love that's free . . .
For love of you and love of Life,
For love that simply dwells in me . . .
I'll see it through with laughter
And with mystery and majesty;
For I am sister to the man
And I am sister to the Moon
But to witches I am Queen, you see,
And holder of the Sword and Key!

. . .

### II

. . .

And I have a sacred oath as well
To set the wizard in you free
And have you understand . . .
That all you had to do was live this long!
Was to fight to be so soft and strong;
Was to pass the harshest,
most unyielding test
Of trusting that you could be blest
To walk differently to all the rest!

. . .

I see you in the Forest deep
Wild rose and mosses at your feet
And mists, like ghosts, between huge
trees . . .
I see you gently bend your knees
And kiss the earth with lips and tears . . .

—from *The Feast of Flesh & Spirit* by Ly de Angeles

## AUTHOR'S NOTE

*"Bring me my broadsword and clear understanding . . ."*

Today is the 26th of May, 1998, and this country is having a National "Sorry" Day because generations of the children of Australia's indigenous people were stolen from their families and forced to grow up in "good Christian missions," in "decent, white-man's clothes" with the grandiose idea that they would be better off.

The current commonwealth government will not say, "Gee, guys, our forefathers were bastards! We know better. We're sorry, so sorry, for what was done to you and it won't happen again." Although people from all over this land, from all backgrounds, do concede the inhumanity perpetrated against the Aboriginal Nation, holistically, the government does not (methinks they dare not!). There is an entire agenda occurring off center stage, like at Jabiluka, tribal land currently being mined for yellow-cake, the authorities arresting the rightful owners of this sacred site for trespass, while they seek to eradicate native title and perpetuate a race election to divide us, in true Machiavellian fashion, further!

Since the invasion of this continent by the British two hundred years ago, ethnogenocide has been waged against the tribal communities. Like apartheid in South Africa, the Black & Tans in Ireland, and the Holocaust of the Second World War, these events are not events that should be forgotten, because forgetting can lead to the sleep of freedom.

It happened to us.

Not just witches, but heretics of all backgrounds who were not in accord with the agenda of the dominant, current regime. Not just witches, but an entire multi-indigenous culture—the inhabitants of the British Isles before the invasion of the bloody

Roman Empire. The annihilation of the history, equality, legend, music, art, language, religion, tradition, and inheritance of a tribal people—the sins of the father. If you were not Roman, you were no one. People were bought, humiliated, absorbed, or slaughtered. Rebels fought, and fought, and ran away to live to fight another day. For centuries.

Then, after Constantine hedged his bets and declared Christianity to be the religion of the state, the second wave to overthrow the ways of the sacred began. The last attempts (even of a Celtic Christianity) of individuality were quashed as a result of the Synod of Whitby in 664 C.E. The pursuit and eradication of the heretics (from the Greek *hairetikos*: able to choose!) of an older faith were dealt with "by way of a hostile sword" (Bede).

The ways of the ancients (outwardly, and in the majority) were blanketed. Our feast days were overwritten by Christian saints' days or Christian holy days. Singing, the playing of music, dancing, and learning were outlawed, as was the tattooing of the clans and their sorcerers (who became the property of the Crown and, in this country, today, are still considered outlaw). Hedge schools, the ways of teaching the young by the Druids, was outlawed, as was the recanting of tribal lineage and legacy by the Bards.

The British became an empire riding on the traditions of ownership, war, and accumulation that were Roman in origin, and they have perpetuated the dysfunction on every tribal people of every land they have invaded since (even, still, in Ireland).

How can a people forget? Do they forget? It is unsafe to remember; it is unsafe to let their children know; it is too horrendous to carry the grief of that heavy, and complete, a defeat for too many generations; it is safer, better, to let it all go and to be granted the handouts and boons from the dominant regime. There seems to be safety in numbers, just as there seems to be safety in anonymity—the suit and tie, the nice, neat dress with matching accessories in the acceptable mode of the population, the subservience of women, the ownership of children, the segregation and ostracizing of those who will not be absorbed into the common dye.

The Stones still stand to remind us—they didn't pull them down. Why? Because if they'd pulled down all the Henges and they'd eradicated the Sheila na gig from the church lintels and the Green Man from above the tavern door, possibly no one would remember, and the people would not deduce that theirs is an inheritance of magic that exists from before the unacceptability of passion became the norm. The secret will of the soul of a people is why!

All things come full circle.

Not only the Stones, but the song within our blood.

This book is not only the way I live in the Way of witch, it is my inheritance (which is my humanity, inherently magical!). In one way, it was written so that others who need to know this kind of magic can live it also, having another witch's opinions to assist them, but, the truth be told, it is the power of the individual, it is *the honor of differences* that I seek to perpetuate—my difference, your difference—that's why I have never said "you have to," ever, in this work.

In secrecy and in mystery, and behind the veils of sacred ritual, the people *do* remember! There's no reason at all why the tapestry of different thought, passion, and faith cannot live in symphony, each honoring the instrument of the other.

A few years ago, I had my face tattooed with the symbols of deep meaning that mean everything to me. I did so because I had come to the turning point that we all, sooner or later, approach—how much do I care to be acceptable to those who are not of my kind to the detriment of the truth of my commitment? I did it for my mother, and for her mother, and for hers—for as far back as time remembers—and I felt them all there with me, the songline of my ancestors who dare not, for the sake of their children, and the children who came after, make magic obvious.

This book is for (in order of age) Adam, Jarrod, and Serenity, children of my body, who keep me true to myself, and for each of my initiates and those who have trained in the collectives (outer circle), children of another kind of mother . . . ad infinitum.

# END NOTES

1.  From *The Sea Priestess* by Dion Fortune.

2.  Conscience—from the Latin *conscire*, meaning "to know inwardly."

3.  I italicize the word because the *misunderstanding*, in and of itself, will be illusory. You can be very clear and concise in communication, and when you no longer play by the rules of the anticipated roles that you have set up for yourself so that you will be considered acceptable, then you may often be misunderstood.

4.  See Ethics of Personal Power in Section One.

5.  I have italicized the word *belief* because, in my opinion, inherent within the word is the word "doubt."

6.  Biocide—late twentieth-century word associated with the slaughter of biodiversity for unjustifiable wealth—the current god of a rationalist culture.

7.  *Geas* is an antique witch's term for something like "the raven that sits and whispers on my shoulder," something that is one's destiny to pursue.

8.  See both sections on Mulengro to assist in this aspect of your training.

9.  See The Ethics of Personal Power, Part One, Section Two.

10. Regarding active and passive silence, active silence is the use of manifest, background sound (e.g., music, thunderstorms when they are around, the wind in the trees, the ocean's song) as an aid; passive silence is silence without sound.

11. For more indepth information, see Dreamwalker, Part Three.

12. Freefalling, in Witchcraft, is where one allows changes to occur at random in alignment with a desire to feel a certain way when circumstances are aligned accordingly.

13. This is the practice of summoning called *evocation* rather than invocation.

14. See The Law of Congruity, Part One, Section Two.

15. See Mulengro, this section.

16. See The Art of Invisibility, Part Three.

17. See Glamouring, Part Three

18. Read *The Moon Under Her Feet* by C. Kinstler, and *The Women's Encyclopedia of Myths and Secrets* by Barbara G. Walker.

# Section Two

# REFERENCES

## PLANETARY SYMBOLISM

**Sun:** ☉ Center of the self. Symbolism: spiritual flame. Represents your purpose of being along the timescape of your destiny. It is the principle of self-actualization. It is your essence, and therefore your will to be (as in becoming) and your ability to create and express yourself as an individual. It is expansive and electric, but it can tend to blind you to the subtleties of the diversity of nature, both individually and collectively. It is fortissimo.

*On the Tree of Life, ☉ is the Assiatic association of Tiphareth, which dwells at the heart of the Ruach and is linked, like an eight-spoked wheel, to all facets of the Tree. It is linked (through Da'ath) to Kether ♆, ♇; Chokmah ♅, Binah ♄, Chesed ♃, Geburah ♂, Hod ☿, Netzach ♀, Yesod ☽ directly.*

**Moon:** ☽ The Moon receives and reflects the Sun's rays and light. It represents the cycles of change; ebb and flow; the tides of both the individual and the collective. It is both contractive and magnetic, blatant and occult. It is the facility that endows you with your intuitive/psychic faculty, that determines how the energies of the self are used. It indicates the subconscious mind and is also the matrix image of your being. It connects you to both your genetic and instinctual memories. It is the source of adaptability and the instincts of self-preservation.

*On the Tree of Life, ☽ represents the Assiah of Yesod, which is linked to Tiphareth ☉, Hod ☿, Netzach ♀, and Malkuth ⊗ directly.*

**Mercury:** ☿ The conscious mind and the workings of the conscious mind. Mercury endows you with your basic attitudes toward your interactive environment. It rules communication on a contact level (to extend yourself into your environment via communication of your identity). It endows the expression of perceptions with an intelligence through the spoken and/or written word. It rules the sciences, movement and magic, logic and learning. Mercury is the quality of thought as distinct from the quantity, and the ability to focus thought and direct it toward application.

*On the Tree of Life, ☿ represents Hod, which is linked to Geburah ♂, Tiphareth ☉, Netzach ♀, Yesod ☽, and Malkuth ⊗ directly.*

**Venus:** ♀ Venus gives form to what Mercury produces in concept. It is the deciding factor in the laws of attraction and repulsion. It is fecund, sensual, nourishing, artistic, and aesthetic. It is also that which establishes the essential values in your life. Venus represents the senses, that which is sensate and sensitive—all cognitive capacity to respond to what is felt.

*On the Tree of Life, ♀ represents the Assiah of Netzach, which is linked to Chesed ♃, Tiphareth ☉, Hod ☿, Yesod ☽, and Malkuth ⊗ directly.*

**Mars:** ♂ Mars indicates your basic excitations and the quality of initiative and decisive action. It denotes your aggression and your striving nature. It is responsible for your directed sexuality, your familial, tribal, communal, and cultural affiliations. It is your sense of justice and your concept of taboo. It is your capacity to defend. Mars rules the muscles and all physical energy. It is your powerful, aggressive preservation instinct, and it is more social than personal.

*On the Tree of Life, ♂ represents the Assiah of Geburah and is linked to Binah ♄, Chesed ♃, Tiphareth ☉, and Hod ☿ directly.*

**Jupiter:** ♃ Jupiter represents your basic capacity for expansion, idealism, and compassion in any given endeavor. It also represents your ability to improve yourself through education (in this respect, it is polarized with Mercury). Jupiter governs conditioned and ingrained traditional philosophies, judgments, and morals—from religious affiliations to political preferences. It also pertains to the devotional aspects of the self, and one's awareness of what is personally and collectively sacred. It is how you *are* in a public sense, rather than a private one.

*On the Tree of Life, ♃ represents the Assiah of Chesed, and is linked to Chokmah ♅, Geburah ♂, Tiphareth ☉, and Netzach ♀ directly.*

**Saturn:** ♄ Saturn defines your limitations. (This planet has been so maligned due to a misunderstanding of its deeper nature, that I would like to quote the mathematical meaning of the term limit: a definite quantity or value that a

series is conceived or proved to approach but *never reach*.
The italics are mine.). It relates to your concrete creative faculties and is the crystallization of the Sun's (in this instance,
our personal star) energies (the self). It represents all concepts of conditioning, as well as conditioning itself, both in
yourself and in society as a whole. It presents you with the
awareness of binding and restriction, as well as being that
which is both binding and restricting. It is there to give you
the opportunity *to break through the immobilization of your
own limitations.* Saturn symbolizes that which is ordered,
ancient, deep, and profound. It is achievement within the
acceptable cultural paradigm of present-day society, based on
long-standing traditions of what constitutes success. Qabbal-
istically, Saturn represents Binah, the Great Sea, Almah
Mari. On the outward journey of the Lightning Flash, Binah
is where force (Chokmah), which is pure, unbridled, and
unrecognizable energy, has entered into the dimension of
time to be able to know itself. It arcs, and turns back on itself
in order to recognize itself; hence life, the galaxies, and everything that *is* within space (the theory of relativity, after
another fashion: time is to space, as matter is to energy).

*On the Tree of Life, ♄ represents the Assiah of Binah and is
directly linked to Kether ♆, ♀, to Chokmah ♅ (through Da'ath),
Geburah ♂, and Tiphareth ☉.*

**Chiron:** ⚷ Chiron is the way through. It is between Saturn ♄,
which relates to restriction, and Uranus ♅, which influences
vision before action. It is the gateway for the psyche's libera-
tion; for the release (hence the transformation) of the spirit
from the confines of perceived limitations based on the ways
of others. It is where the pupil surpasses the teacher and the
teaching. It is the dissatisfaction that leads to both inner and

manifest rebellion. The Chiron influence is not a quality with which you are born, but rather that which develops through an active involvement in social and cultural affairs. It is that which endows you with a sense of responsibility *other* than that which society expects. It indicates the darkness prior to initiation. It is the avenue through which you may seek a deeper meaning to life, which leads, thence, to a transcendent vision (Uranus). Its emphasis is on the expansive mind over and beyond the rational mind.

*On the Tree of Life, it represents Da'ath, or the bridge above (or that veils) the abyss. Da'ath represents knowledge not necessarily gained from a recognizable source (i.e., inspiration that leads to discovery), and it links Chokmah ⛢ to Binah ♄ on the path of the Lightning Flash, and Kether ♆, ♇ with Tiphareth ☉ by way of the High Priestess card, which broaches the abyss.*

**Uranus:** ⛢ Uranus, Neptune, and Pluto are known collectively as Ambassadors of the Galaxy. Uranus relates to the vision you can have beyond and above recognized traditional norms. Uranus is that which breaks down the walls of accepted standards and deconditions the personal ego. It will lead you into situations that will shatter preconceived ideas you may have of yourself, established by your socio/environmental upbringing. It can be like the lightning-struck tower in the Tarot insofar as its eruptive and destructive blatancy can be as dangerous as exposed electrical wiring to wet hands in a thunderstorm! It is, however, the power of the urge for differentiation and the revolution of independent consciousness, and it is characterized by the expression mental vision.

*On the Tree of Life, ⛢ represents Chokmah in its Assiatic expression, and it links with Kether ♆, ♇, Binah ♄, Chesed ♃, and thence to Tiphareth ☉, directly.*

**Neptune:** ♆ Neptune has been termed the Universal Solvent. Whatever Uranus has destroyed, Neptune dissolves. It has a great deal to do with your faith in what is happening when radical feelings are concerned and when changes occur through them. It indicates your resonant feelings relative to humanity as a whole. Neptune rules mysticism and the urge to propel yourself deeper and deeper past the gateway of normal thought. It rules the more sacred feelings and lateral views on spirituality, and is characterized by the phrase "visionary feeling."

*On the Tree of Life, ♆ represents the Assiah of Kether and is linked to Chokmah ♅, Binah ♄, and Tiphareth ☉ (through Da'ath) directly.*

**Pluto:** ♇ What's left of you after Uranus and Neptune have had their go at you is what Pluto is all about! All concepts of a spiritual nature are pulverized onto a screen, on which is projected your new image. Pluto relates to the transcendence and transformation of your life-pattern boundaries. It is the action that is a result of the *mental* of Uranus and the *feeling* of Neptune. It is, therefore, the Planet of Enlightenment.

*On the Tree of Life, ♇ dwells on the lip, or at the point of the unknown, where Kether becomes Ain Soph Aur, therefore indicating another Tree (an unperceived reality). One could speculate that this is Malkuth ⊗, after another fashion, in which an entire Tree springs from the death of the fruits of the Tree that it was, is, and ever will be, through the seed that is born from Pluto's promise.*

You can use these interpretations in just about any way you choose. Contemplate their significance to you, personally, to understand the passages of the pattern of your own life. Comprehending the planetary symbolism by way of the Tree of Life is a great *secret of weaving*. Understand the qualities of each planet in relation to your own nature to enable you to work magic according to your own nature (i.e., the line of least resistance).

## TAROT (MAJOR ARCANA)

I have been asked on many occasions to produce a book, or a how-to manual, teaching Tarot, as I have taught the subject to many people over the past fifteen years, but what I teach is not static. Tarot, particularly as a tool of divination (which is its purpose, as far as I am concerned), is the epitome of malleability! Prediction requires the presentation of many patterns, or groupings, throughout a reading, using all seventy-eight cards. The value of each individual card is dependent on those cards it is grouped with. Basically, the seventy-eight cards are like seventy-eight letters, the groupings are like sentences, and the whole of a reading is the telling of a story that is inherent in an individual's destiny, different for each individual. How can that be put down in a book and be even remotely credible?

If I were to read the same story for everyone (variations of a theme being the dominant paradigm), then perhaps—but it's *not* that way; it is never that way. I can explain *how* it works and *why* it works now that I have a handle on the principles of quantum physics (wherein lies Tarot's secret, as it *does* defy the laws of probability), and I can teach small groups of dedicated students how to interpret the language of patterns—but by word of mouth, always by word of mouth.

What is the probability ratio of the patterns Tarot exhibits in one reading? In one reading alone there will be distinct series of information, based on pattern, that will be repeated over and over, with variations relative to each experience that one person will have (in the case of my readings, that will generally cover an approximate two-year interval). Names, places, dates, and descriptions of experiences not based on the person's current situation are often given, and they *do* occur, often word-for-word. No one could record each and every story they read, for several thousand people, in any one book, and teaching to read the language orally and experientially (which is what students of the Tarot learn) can really be achieved only through personal interaction.

Therefore, the notes written here have *nothing* to do with divination in its foretelling aspect (I would require you in my class for that). These notes are oracular, and therefore of benefit to both the psyche and to spellcrafting based on emotion and ideal.

Each Major Arcanum has a planetary, elemental, or zodiacal association stemming from its connection to la Rose Croix, and the value of these associations is to be contemplated, as it can be of great assistance in seeking to understand each card's significance. I'm presenting you with a contemplation of each principle, and though each principle may very well be the answer to a question of importance to your development or the development of an endeavor, it could also simply be a time sequence, yet to come, based on an experience, yet to come, whereby the answer will be forthcoming. Tarot very definitely deals with time, but in time's unfolding sense of an ever-present continuum (i.e., past, present, and future being what the Aboriginal people of this land call a *songline*).

The Major Arcana can also be experienced in a ritualized sense, as pathworking. The twenty-two cards form a holistic experience of birth, life, and death (revolutionarily speaking). This is known as The Fool's Journey. The Fool Card (0) is really the Divine Fool, and represents the walking-of-the-wheel, seemingly blindly, for the sake of the experience of living. (Reading an already read story is never quite the same as doing it the first time—you already know the characters, the plot, and the punchline! What's the point?) Therefore, the *package* of one's destiny is in a constant state of unfolding. The Fool can be said to be the only card in the pack, holding the other seventy-seven cards in immanence in his little bundle. This is the weirdness of Tarot as a tool of divination—the experience you will have in the future, have already been "done" in a reading, could be said to be an experience of the past!

# TIME

My grandmother came to live with my mother, my sister, and me when I was eleven years old. She read cards and tea leaves, and there was always someone secreted away with her in her little room at the back of the house "gettin' done." She was so good! She could give you names, dates, places, and times. She even knew, a week before her death, that my mother was going to go through grief between Saturday (which was when my grand-mother had a massive cerebral hemorrhage resulting in body-death the following morning) and Tuesday (which was when she was cremated). She was my original "guiding light," and her ways well and truly triggered my lifescape.

She explained the way of time to me, when I was young, like this: "Let's say you're living on a sphere. Let's say the only things of significance on the sphere are a bloody big door in a bloody big door frame in the middle of nowhere with a path that leads away from that door in a dead-straight line. Let's say the door's behind you and your feet are on that path, and you decide to walk it to see where it goes, 'cause there doesn't seem to be much of anything else to do.

"So you walk that path for a long time, and lots might happen to you while you're walking it, but, sure thing is, you end up behind that bloody big door. What I want you to ask yourself is: when you walk through that door, close it, and stand on the other side looking out at the path in front of you, are you in your past? Are you in the present? Or is it the future you've just walked into? Or is it maybe all three at once and it's just the journey that mucks you up in the head about it all?" (She was an Aquarian. Her birthday, interestingly enough, was February 2).

That's it, yes?

# Major Arcana

0   The Fool        △   The essence; the concept or
                        inspiration; prelife; the unpre-
                        dictable; inevitability; destiny;
                        the principle of the whole being
                        greater than the sum of its
                        parts.

Here begins the first phase of the Fool's journey . . .

I   Magician        ☿   Force taking form; the first
                        primal action; creation and
                        creator; all things potent; the
                        power of one; "in the beginning
                        . . ."; the adept; an absolute
                        refusal of betrayal.

II  High Priestess  ☽   The mystery veiled; the veil
                        itself; law; guardianship; life
                        unseen; silence; the occultist
                        and the priestess; the profundity
                        of the Unknown.

III Empress         ♀   The result of action; glory in
                        life; growth through action;
                        fecundity; the fertile thought
                        gives nourishment if
                        propagated; the rampant
                        nature of the continuum.

IV  Emperor         ♈   Competence through
                        experience; authority (balanced
                        or unbalanced); an externalized
                        expression of will and power
                        within the lifescape; control for
                        a reason.

| | | | |
|---|---|---|---|
| V | Hierophant | ♉ | Mystical guidance; if restricted, it is divisionist, dogmatic, bigoted, pompous, or pragmatic; when free, it is spiritual creativity and union with the gods; grace. |
| VI | Lovers | ♊ | The crossroads of thought and ideal, direction and destiny, union or dispersion, action or nonaction; choice and all that is engendered by choice; the symbol of a triangle. |
| VII | Chariot | ♋ | Transcendence of the self over mundane entrapment; attainment and self-assurance through perseverance; the battle of life's trial won, but not the war; victory! |
| VIII | Strength | ♌ | Inner force and power through consistency; the knowledge that harassment achieves nothing, neither does it create; inner power, outer tranquillity; indomitability; rich, deep, intractable power; the power of peaceful revolution; the concept of "stare that beastie in the face and really give 'em hell!" (from Jethro Tull's *Broadsword and the Beast* album). |

| IX | Hermit | ♍ | The solitude inherent in one's own becoming; the cloak of the secret; inner wisdom and endurance through despair being the guiding light of one's destiny; the power of a sacred aspiration and the separation that it engenders; no compromise; the knowledge that one's life journey can be shared, but is ultimately traveled alone. |
| X | Wheel of Fortune | ♃ | Situations that cannot be controlled; day-to-day-to-day-to-day; heaven and hell; a testing of boredom; a challenge of patience; the lull; becalmed; landlocked; deeper forces ally with the surface to assess the soul through mere circumstances; Question: What's the best way to make god laugh? Answer: Tell him your plans! |
| XI | Justice | ♎ | Following through into action with an ideal; assessment by the soul's judges; compassion by the sword; the fine-honed, razor-sharp steel—the process of tempering by adversity; determined awareness; impartiality to external coercion; the point of balance; your oaths and your contracts of agreement. |

The end of the first phase of the Fool's journey.

The initiation of the Fool's journey into the dark night of the soul.

| XII | Hanged Man | ▽ | Clear and absolute faith in your convictions; the demands from the depths of the soul; sacrifice of safety because of a greater love; willingness to be true to what you know to be right action in the face of overwhelming opposition; the illusion becomes the illumined; the testing of trust, and trust itself; honor; the grail quest and the love of Shekinah; letting go. |

First phase in the Fool's journey through the dark night of the soul.

| XIII | Death | ♏ | Completion (so far); becoming what you have aspired to become; transformation and transformation through initiation; the end and what that really indicates; the fulfillment of a series or a pattern of the lifescape; the center of a maze; the fulfillment of a specific quest. |

Second phase of the Fool's journey through the dark night of the soul.

XIV   Temperance        ♐        The alchemy of any endeavor,
                                 and the alchemist; tightrope-
                                 walking through the dark
                                 night of the soul; the
                                 balancing-act of ingredients in
                                 the lifescape; leftover,
                                 unresolved issues threaten the
                                 balance; the ego undergoing
                                 strident discipline through
                                 experiences; new ideas
                                 surround and influence,
                                 testing one's resolve; tread
                                 carefully, aim carefully; not too
                                 heavy, but not too light either;
                                 mutable.

Third phase of the Fool's journey through the dark night of
the soul.

XV   Devil             ♑        Self-entrapment; the face of
                                 pompous self-contentment;
                                 false and true knowledge; a
                                 trap; an adversary; the dross of
                                 old, outmoded confusion; the
                                 threat of danger; either/or
                                 morality; self-righteousness;
                                 fear-consciousness; unaccept-
                                 able situations that you refuse
                                 to let go of through lack of self-
                                 alliance; "There's a beast upon
                                 your shoulder, and there's a
                                 fiend upon your back . . ."
                                 (from Jethro Tull's *Broadsword
                                 and the Beast* album).

Fourth phase of the Fool's journey through the dark night of the soul.

| XVI Tower | ♂ | The-shit-hits-the-fan; apparent destruction; circumstances test the resolve; if the "I am" has become the "better than you," now face the consequences; questioning reality; devastation; disaster; "I see a dark sail on the horizon set under a black cloud that hides the sun" (from Jethro Tull's *Broadsword and the Beast* album); humiliation. |

This completes the Fool's journey through the dark night of the soul. Here begins the second phase of the Fool's journey—the true child. The Fool's conscious conception . . .

| XVII Star | ♒ | Realization; sight; vision; in touch with a vast wisdom; tranquillity confirms beauty, both within and without; clear understanding; the long journey from here to there; light, enlightenment, and the light at the end of the tunnel. |

The Fool's maturation in the Dragon's Egg . . .

XVIII Moon                  ♓        Intuition brings illumination of
                                     the hidden dark places for
                                     deeper understanding of the
                                     true nature of both the
                                     biological and transcendental
                                     nature of the individual,
                                     though sometimes "through a
                                     glass darkly"; acceptance of the
                                     wild as well as the controlled;
                                     the inner self is aware of
                                     deception and needs deny its
                                     influence; acceptance of the
                                     primal instincts disguised
                                     behind the veneer of so-called
                                     civilizational sophistication; a
                                     rich understanding of the
                                     rhythms and patterns of biodi-
                                     versity.

The Fool is born as the child who is its own parent . . .

XIX   Sun                   ☉        Achievement; success; absolute
                                     individual beauty; the
                                     knowledge that who you have
                                     sought to be you have, in actu-
                                     ality, become; discovering won-
                                     der; inner trust; simple truth;
                                     the Zen koan "before
                                     enlightenment, chop wood,
                                     carry water; after enlighten-
                                     ment, chop wood, carry water;"
                                     dawn in the desert; the princi-
                                     ple of the word "principle."

XX   Judgment              △        Rebirth, rebirth, rebirth;
                                    change in accordance with
                                    one's pattern, and one's pattern
                                    being allied with one's will;
                                    understanding what death is,
                                    as well as what it isn't;
                                    freedom: true freedom requires
                                    eternal vigilance; art rather
                                    than reproductionism—the
                                    principle of creation.

The Fool's journey is complete thus far . . .

XXI   World                ♄        You've spent so long seeking to
                                    become free of limitations, just
                                    to realize you need your own
                                    personal, self-chosen bound-
                                    aries!; experience reveals itself
                                    as spiral-like; revolution; being
                                    *in* the world but not *of* it—
                                    where is the Fool now?;
                                    understanding that universe
                                    simply means "one song," and
                                    that there are countless songs
                                    and countless singers;
                                    understanding the beauty in
                                    the ordinary; the wider arc of
                                    Binah's gate: understanding;
                                    unity expressed in the
                                    multiplicity of individuality;
                                    home.

   The Fool's journey begins another revolution in the great
wheel. Tarot begins again, but after another fashion—it will be
different the next time and the next.

# The Time Sequences of the Solar/Earth Wheel (According to the Major Arcana)

The following dates are generalized. You would need to refer to an ephemeris for the exact dates in each calendar year.

Aries      Emperor (with the Page of Wands)
March 22–April 21

Taurus      Empress (with the Page of Pentacles)
April 22–May 21

Gemini      Lovers (with the Page of Swords)
May 22–June 21

Cancer      Chariot (with the Page of Cups)
June 22–July 21

Leo      Strength (with the Page of Wands)
July 22–August 21

Virgo      Hermit (with the Page of Pentacles)
August 22–September 21

Libra      Justice (with the Page of Swords)
September 22–October 21

Scorpio      Death (with the Page of Cups)
October 22–November 21

Sagittarius      Temperance (with the Page of Wands)
November 22–December 21

Capricorn      Devil (with the Page of Pentacles)
December 22–January 21

Aquarius      Star (with the Page of Swords)
January 22–February 21

Pisces                    Moon (with the Page of Cups)
                          February 22–March 21

# NUMBER SYMBOLISM

Numerology is the science that concludes that because all things are vibrational, they can be reduced to numbers (equations, sets of symbols representing particle, probability, or potential), and that all numbers can be reduced to a single value, 1 through 9 (the exceptions being 11, 22, and 33 as significant to the concept of indirect effect of an esoteric principle).

Note: the numbers 1 through 9 represent the Sephiroth of the Tree of Life—Kether and Malkuth being representations of each other insofar as 10 is 1 born into a new phase of itself! 11 and 33 are subjective, and therefore relate to Da'ath, and 22 represents the objective paths linking each aspect of the collective Sephiroth.

The exercise here is to consider each number and expand on the concept by putting pen to paper, using your own experiences to guide you to expanded contexts; and to understand how each conceptualized number pertains to your life, both experientially and mystically. I have reduced the meanings of each number to their finest potency and expressed them as key words.

Please contemplate.

| 1 | I am | Individuality, independence, innovation |
| 2 | I share | Cooperation, rhythm, sensitivity, interaction |
| 3 | I express | Communication, self-expression, optimism |
| 4 | I build | System, hard work, power through routine |
| 5 | I change | Change, adaptability, freedom, movement |

| 6 | I comfort | Nurturing, service, healing, compassion |
| 7 | I seek | Analysis, introspection, philosophy, mysticism |
| 8 | I accumulate | Financial acumen, organization, structure |
| 9 | I feel | Philanthropy, wisdom, aloneness, nonpermanency, a lack of clear boundaries |
| 11 | I accept | The dreamer, visionary, needs grounding |
| 22 | I expand | Takes from establishment and creates change |
| 33 | We are one | No clear sense of individuality, can be devastating in our current materialistic climate |

To relate to these concepts at all, it is first necessary to understand how they relate to you personally (hence, collectively). I have included a condensed layout of a numerology chart for you to work with (a fully descriptive discussion relative to this subject would fill a book).

## Exercise

1. Write the name that you were first officially given (i.e., on your birth certificate.) Any subsequent name changes can be taken into account as secondary information only. Your first legal name is some kind of weird Assiatic contract between you and your unfolding lifescape.

2. Equate each letter of your entire name (i.e., first, any middle, and last names as per your birth certificate) with its corresponding letter as shown in the following chart (using your own name in place of the example).

## Alphanumeric Conversion Chart

| 1 | 2 | 3 | 4 | 5 | 6 | 7 | 8 | 9 | | 11 | 22 | 33 |
|---|---|---|---|---|---|---|---|---|---|----|----|----|
| A | B | C | D | E | F | G | H | I | | • | • | • |
| J | • | L | M | N | O | P | Q | R | | K | • | • |
| S | T | U | • | W | X | Y | Z | • | | • | V | • |

The total of all the numbers in your whole name are reduced to a base number by adding the digits. This number gives you the Total Self. You also need to equate your Soul Self by way of the breakdown system using only the vowels, including the letter Y, and your Personality, which is discovered by way of the breakdown of the consonants. Example:

```
J A N E     M A R Y     S M I T H
1 1 5 5     4 1 9 7     1 4 9 2 8
   12/(3)       21/(3)       24/(6) = 57/(12) = 3: Total Self
```

Vowels Only Plus Y

```
J A N E     M A R Y     S M I T H
  1   5       1   7         9
      6           8         9  = 23 = 5: Soul Self
```

Consonants Only

```
J A N E     M A R Y     S M I T H
  1 5         4   9       1 4   2 8
      6          13/(4)      15/(6) = 34/(16) = 7: Personality
```

3.  The first letter of your first name is called the *foundation*, which is the harmonic of power that supports who you are.

4.  The total of the letters of your first name is called your *key*, and the properties of this number aid you in interrelationships.

5.  Problem areas in your psyche are indicated by whatever numbers are missing from your name (in the case of our example, these numbers are: 3, 5, and 6. Using the chart, we can see that missing 3 means a lack of clear ability to express herself; missing 5 means a dysfunctional attitude toward change; and missing 6 indicates difficulties in mutual relationships.

6.  Cycles of time are decided from your date of birth. Set out your information as in the following example:

    Date of birth: June 5, 1922
    $$6 \quad 5 \quad 14/(5) = 25/(16) = 7: \textbf{Destiny}$$

7.  You have three Saturn cycles in your life. The number symbolism for each is determined as follows:

    **0–29 years:** the first Saturn Cycle, taken from the month of your birth.

    **29–56 years:** the second Saturn Cycle, taken from the day of your birth.

    **56 years onward:** the third Saturn Cycle, taken from the year of your birth.

8.  To evaluate your personal year (beginning from your last birthday, and ending the day before your next birthday), add the day and month of your birthday with the calendar year of your last birthday. Example for Jane Mary Smith:

    June 5, 1998 (calendar year of last birthday)
    $$6 \quad 5 \quad 27/(9) = 20/(11) = \textbf{2: Current Personal Year}$$

You now have the following information:

Total Self = 3

Soul Self = 5

Personality = 7

Foundation = 1

Key = 3

Recommendations for Strengthening = 3, 5, 6

Destiny = 7

First Saturn Cycle = 6

Second Saturn Cycle = 5

Third Saturn Cycle = 5

Current Personal Year = 2

It is not necessary to have an extensive numerology chart drawn up unless you desire. If you feel that this is what you want to do, there are many books available on the subject, some of which utilize a technique similar to this; some are utterly different. My experience has shown that this system is admirable, in both its simple and expanded states (about twenty typewritten pages long!).

What is most important is that you use the tools of understanding, oracle, and divination with caution, never seeking to use them as an excuse to deny free will.

## Table of Correspondences: The Elements

| Element | Elemental | Tarot | Zodiacal | Planetary | Color | Plant | Direction |
|---------|-----------|-------|----------|-----------|-------|-------|-----------|
| Fire | Salamander | Wands | Aries, Leo, Sagittarius | Mars, Sun, Jupiter | Red (and all assoc. colors) | Nettle | North in the S. Hem.; South in the N. Hem. |
| Water | Undine | Cups | Cancer, Scorpio, Pisces | Moon, Pluto, Neptune | Green (and all assoc. colors) | Lotus (all water plants) | West |
| Earth | Gnomes | Pentacles | Taurus, Virgo, Capricorn | Venus, Mercury, Saturn | Black, brown (and all assoc. colors) | Red poppy | South in the S. Hem.; North in the N. Hem. |
| Air | Sylphs | Swords | Gemini, Libra Aquarius | Mercury, Venus, Uranus | Blue, yellow (and all assoc. colors) | Aspen, mistletoe | East |

# Table of Correspondences: Planetary Symbols

| Planet | Color | Plant | Metal | Gem | Perfume | Day | Creature |
|---|---|---|---|---|---|---|---|
| Sun | Yellow, gold | Sunflower, mistletoe, heliotrope, goldenrod, oak, blessed thistle, saffron, bay | Gold | Topaz, yellow diamond | Olibanum, wood-aloes, cinnamon | Sunday | Lion, phoenix, eagle, stag, gorilla, shark, salmon, kangaroo |
| Moon | Violet, silver | Almond, willow, lavender, violet, hazel, henbane, cohosh, foxglove, mandrake | Silver | Quartz crystal, moonstone | Camphor, jasmine | Monday | Elephant, owl, toad, hare, bat, spider, stingray |
| Mercury | Orange | Vervain, styrax, cinquefoil, alder, morning glory, aspen | Quicksilver, cinnabar | Agate, amber | Narcissus, storax | Wednesday | Jackal, twinserpents, lizard, fox, dolphin, sylphs, salamanders |
| Venus | Green | Myrtle, fennel, apple, yarrow, rose, gardenia, wattle, pennyroyal | Copper | Emerald, jade | Ambergris, lotus, gardenia, rose | Friday | Lynx, cat, dove, wolf, cow, bear, shellfish, nymphs, dryads |
| Mars | Scarlet | Absinthe, rue, poplar, thorn, hawthorn, ginger, peppercorn, wolfsbane | Iron, pyrite | Ruby, carnelian, black-boy plant, resin | Sulphur, tobacco, dragon's blood, | Tuesday | Basilisk, man, crow, adder, king brown snake, vulture, echidna, seagull, baboon, boar |

## Table of Correspondences: Planetary Symbols, continued

| Planet | Color | Plant | Metal | Gem | Perfume | Day | Creature |
|---|---|---|---|---|---|---|---|
| Jupiter | Royal blue | Agrimony, rue, olive, elm, woad, cedar, sage, rosemary, Solomon's seal | Tin | Sapphire, lapis lazuli | Aloes, balm, sandalwood, frankincense | Thursday | Centaur, unicorn, dog, horse, buffalo, albatross, hawk, Tuatha de Dannan |
| Saturn | Indigo, black, silver | Ash, rowan, indigo, boab, hemlock, holly, fungi, pomegranate, redwood | Lead | Onyx, jet, obsidian | Myrrh, alum, nightqueen | Saturday | Wyvern, woman, raven, black jaguar, crocodile, DNA |
| Uranus | White, flash-blue | Amaranth, sugar cane, white cypress, ghost gum | Uranium, lime | Turquoise | Musk, juniper, benzoin, ozone | — | Gryphon, nephilim, angels, the elven, the atom |
| Neptune | Green/black | Licorice, seaweed | Borax, pumice | Coral | Hemp | — | Nehushtan, whale, turtle, anaconda, mantaray, nixies, kelpies |
| Pluto | Blue/black | Fungi, aniseed, fig, ayahuasca, datura, mesquite | Plutonium, coal | Quartz crystal, diamond | Opium asafoetida | — | Dragon, scorpion, worm, snake, rat, mole, rabbit |

235

# Recommended Reading List

## Non-Fiction

Adler, Margot. *Drawing Down the Moon.* Boston: Beacon Press, 1981.

Ashcroft-Nowicki, Dolores. *First Steps in Ritual,* rev. ed. Wellingborough, UK: Aquarian Press, 1990.

———. *Ritual Magic Workbook.* Wellingborough, UK: Aquarian Press, 1986.

———. *The Shining Paths.* Wellingborough, UK: Aquarian Press, 1983.

———. *The Tree of Ecstasy.* Wellingborough, UK: Aquarian Press.

Baigent, Michael, Richard Leigh, and Henry Lincoln. *Holy Blood, Holy Grail.* New York: Delacorte Press, 1982.

Buckland, Raymond. *Witchcraft From the Inside.* St. Paul, MN: Llewellyn Publications, 1995.

————. *Complete Book of Witchcraft*, St. Paul, MN: Llewellyn Publications, 1987.

Campbell, Joseph. *Occidental Mythology*. New York: Penguin Books, 1982.

————. *Primitive Mythology*. New York: Penguin Books, 1987.

————. *The Hero With a Thousand Faces*, 2d ed. Princeton: University Press, 1968.

Cooper, J. C. *An Illustrated Encyclopedia of Traditional Symbols*, rev. ed. London: Thames & Hudson, 1979.

Crowley, A. *Magick in Theory and Practice*. York Beach, ME: Samuel Weiser Inc., 1973.

Crowley, Vivianne. *Wicca*. London: Thorsons, 1996.

Cunningham, Scott. *Cunningham's Encyclopedia of Magical Herbs*. St. Paul, MN: Llewellyn Publications, 1985.

De Chardin, T. *The Future of Man*. New York: Harper & Row, 1969.

Denning, M. and O. Phillips. *The Sword and the Serpent*. St. Paul, MN: Llewellyn Publications, 1987.

————. *Llewellyn's Practical Guide to Astral Projection*. St. Paul, MN: Llewellyn Publications, 1979.

————. *Llewellyn's Practical Guide to Creative Visualisation*. St. Paul, MN: Llewellyn Publications, 1983.

Drury, Neville. *Don Juan, Mescalito and Modern Magic*. N.p.: Viking, Penguin, 1983.

————. *The Occult Experience*. London: Robert Hale Ltd., 1987.

Estes, Clarissa Pinkola. *Women Who Run With Wolves*. London: Rider, 1992.

Farrar, Stewart and Janet. *Eight Sabbats for Witches*. London: Robert Hale Ltd., 1981.

———. *The Life and Times of a Modern Witch*. Washington: Phoenix, 1988.

Farrar, Stewart. *What Witches Do*. Washington: Phoenix, 1983.

Fortune, Dion. *Mystical Qabalah*. York Beach, ME: Weiser, 1984.

Frazer, James. *The Golden Bough*. 13 vols. London: Macmillan, 1936.

Gleick, James. *Chaos: Making a New Science*. London: Heinemann, 1988.

Graves, Robert. *The White Goddess*. New York: Farrar, Strauss & Giroux, 1966.

Green, M. *Magic for the Aquarian Age*. Wellingborough, UK: Aquarian Press, 1983.

Hall, N. *The Moon and the Virgin*. New York: Harper & Row, 1981.

Harner, Michael. *The Way of the Shaman*. New York: Bantam, 1982.

Hartley, Christine. *The Western Mystery Tradition*. Wellingborough, UK: Aquarian Press, 1986.

Hawking, Stephen. *A Brief History of Time*. London: Bantam, 1988.

Horne, Fiona. *Witch*. Australia: Random House, 1998.

Jung, Carl Gustav. *Man and His Symbols*. New York: Doubleday, 1964.

———. *The Archetypes and the Collective Unconscious*, Vol 1. Princeton, NJ: Princeton University Press.

Kharitidi, Olga. *Entering the Circle: the Secrets of Ancient Siberian Wisdom.* N.p.: HarperCollins, 1996.

Knight, Gareth. *A Practical Guide to Qabbalistic Symbolism.* UK: Helios Books, 1966.

———. *Secret Tradition in Arthurian Legend.* Wellingborough, UK: Aquarian Press, 1983.

Kraig, Donald Michael. *Modern Magick.* St. Paul, MN: Llewellyn Publications, 1989.

Lethbridge, T. C. *Gogmagog.* London: Routledge & Kegan Paul, 1957.

Matt, Daniel C. *The Essential Kabbalah.* San Francisco: Harper-Collins, 1996.

Matthews, John and Caitlin. *The Western Way,* vols. 1 and 2. London: Arcana, 1986.

Matthews, John and Caitlin. *Mabon.* London: Arcana, 1990.

Murray, Margaret. *The God of the Witches.* New York: Oxford University Press, 1973.

Reanney, Darryl. *The Death of Forever.* Australia: Longman Cheshire, 1991.

———. *The Music of the Mind.* Australia: Hill of Content, 1994.

Richardson, Alan. *Gate of Moon,* Wellingborough, UK: Aquarian Press, 1984.

———. *Introduction to the Mystical Qabbalah.* Paths to Inner Power Series. Wellingborough, UK: Aquarian Press, 1987.

Richardson, Alan and Geoff Hughes. *Ancient Magicks for a New Age*. St. Paul, MN: Llewellyn Publications, 1989.

Spence, Lewis. *The Magic Arts in Celtic Britain*. London and New York: Ryder & Co., 1915.

Squire, Charles. *Celtic Myth and Legend*. London: Gresham Publishers, 1905.

Starhawk. *Dreaming the Dark*. Boston: Beacon Press, 1982.

———. *The Spiral Dance*. San Francisco: Harper & Row, 1989.

Stewart, R. J. *Power Within the Land*. Dorset, UK: Element Books, 1992.

Stone, Merlin. *When God Was a Woman*. London: Virago Press, 1976.

Sturzaker, James. *Kabbalistic Aphorisms*, 2d ed. United Kingdom: Metatron, 1981.

Tzu Sun. *The Art of War*. Boston and London: Shambhala, 1988.

Valiente, Doreen. *An ABC of Witchcraft Past and Present*. Washington: Phoenix, 1984.

———. *Natural Magic*. Washington: Phoenix, 1985.

———. *Where Witchcraft Lives*. Wellingborough, UK: Aquarian Press, 1962.

———. *Witchcraft for Tomorrow*. Washington: Phoenix, 1983.

Walker, B. G. *The Women's Encyclopedia of Myths and Secrets*. New York: Harper & Row, 1983.

Warren-Clarke, Ly. *The Way of the Goddess*. Dorset, UK: Prism/Unity Press, 1987. (Out of print, available through interlibrary systems, Australia).

Warren-Clarke, Ly. *The Way of Merlyn*. Dorset, UK: Prism/Unity Press, 1990. (Out of print, available through interlibrary systems, Australia).

## FICTION (CONTEMPORARY FOLKLORE)

Bradley, Marion Zimmer. *Ghostlight*. New York: Tor, 1995.

———. *Gravelight*. New York: Tor, 1997.

———. *Mists of Avalon*. London: Sphere Books, 1984.

———. *Witchlight*. New York: Tor, 1996

Constantine, Storm. *Scenting Hallowed Blood*. London: Signet Books, 1996.

———. *Stalking Tender Prey*. N.p.: Penguin Books, 1995

———. *Stealing Sacred Fire*. N.p.: Penguin Books, 1997.

de Lint, Charles. *Greenmantle*. N.p.: Pan Books, 1992.

———. *Into the Green*. N.p.: Tor Books, 1995.

———. *Memory and Dream*. London: Macmillan, 1994.

———. *Moonheart*. N.p.: Pan Books, 1991.

———. *Someplace to be Flying*. London: Macmillan, 1998.

Flint, Kenneth. *Challenge of the Clans*. London: Bantam Press, 1987.

———. *Champion of the Sidhe*. London: Bantam Press, 1986.

———. *Riders of the Sidhe*. London: Bantam Press, 1987.

Fortune, Dion. *The Goatfoot God*. York Beach, ME: Weiser, 1980.

———. *Moon Magic*. York Beach, ME: Weiser, 1979.

———. *The Sea Priestess*, rev. ed. Wellingborough, UK: Aquarian Press, 1989.

———. *The Secrets of Dr. Tavener*. Georgia: Ariel, 1989.

Holdstock, Robert. *Lavondys*. N.p.: Grafton, 1990.

———. *Mythago Wood*. N.p.: Avon, 1991.

Howard, Robert E. *The Sign of the Moonbow*. Berkeley, CA: Berkeley Publishing, 1977.

Kinstler, Clysta. *The Moon Under Her Feet*. San Francisco: HarperCollins, 1991.

Llywelyn, Morgan. *The Horse Goddess*. Boston: Houghton Mifflin, 1982.

Paxon, Diana L. *The White Raven*. New York: Avon Books, 1989.

Scott, Michael. *Irish Folk and Fairy Tales*. United Kingdom: Warner Books, 1992.

———. *Irish Ghosts and Hauntings*. United Kingdom: Warner Books, 1994.

———. *Irish Myths and Legends*. United Kingdom: Warner Books, 1992.

Starhawk. *The Fifth Sacred Thing*. New York: Bantam Books, 1993.

Watson, Sam. *The Kadaicha Sung*. Australia: Penguin Books, 1990.

Windling, Terri. *The Wood Wife*. United Kingdom: Legend Books, Random House, 1997.

# INDEX

a year and a day, 196

Aboriginal, 123, 202, 216

abraxis, 152

abyss, 133, 213

Adam Kadmon, 70, 122, 124

Aengus Og, 60

altar candle, 71, 91, 93, 96, 100, 140–144, 148–149, 151

amulet, 77, 88, 109–110

angel, 70, 120

apartheid, 202

Aphrodite, 56, 150

Apollo, 60, 123

Aquarius, 70, 227

Aradia, 56, 142–143, 149–150

Arcana, 215–216, 219, 227

Archangelic principle, 69–72

Arianrhod, 56

Aries, 71, 227

art, 6, 36, 42, 49, 53, 73, 79, 81, 84, 110, 119, 152, 157–158, 181, 185, 188, 198, 200, 203, 207, 226

art of invisibility, 181, 207

Artemis, 56, 123

Arthur, 60

Asherah, 56, 122–123

Assiah, 125, 129–134, 194, 210–212, 214

Assiatic, 209, 213, 229

Astarte, 56, 123

astral projection, 147, 153,
    168–169, 171–172

astral travel, 171

astrology, 81, 175

athame, 66, 70, 73–74, 83,
    87–88, 91, 93–98, 100,
    108, 110–111, 140–145,
    148–151, 163, 166–167,
    181–182

Atziluth, 125, 129–134

aura, 154

autumn, 59, 61–63, 72

Autumn Equinox, 61, 63

awareness, 4–5, 10, 12, 37,
    39, 51, 87, 127, 153, 160,
    177, 188, 211–212, 221

Baal, 60

banish, 73, 82, 88–89, 161,
    164, 181–182, 184

banishing, 74, 92, 97, 145,
    151, 161, 163–166, 182,
    184

Baphomet, 60

bards, 203

bathe, 86, 91, 100

Beltaen, 58–59, 63

big bang theory, 126

Binah, 56, 125, 127, 129,
    136, 209, 211–214, 226

bind, 73, 88, 139–140,
    143–144, 146

Black Line, 199–200

blade, 73–74, 93, 95–98,
    110, 144–145, 149

Blessed be, 106, 110–111,
    149, 151, 200

boline, 74, 164

Book of Elements, 20, 25, 27,
    68

Book of Shadows, 78–79,
    99–100, 108, 111, 158

box, 54, 131–132, 138

Briah, 125, 129–133

Brigantia, 56

Brigid, 56

Cancer, 72, 227

candle, 8, 21, 71, 91, 93, 96,
    100, 140–145, 148–149,
    151, 163, 183, 190

candlesticks, 76

Capricorn, 69, 227

cards, 215–217

casting, 87, 90, 92, 166

cauldron, 72

censer, 75–76, 91, 93–94, 96, 140, 143–144, 148, 151, 163, 181

centaur, 152

center, 3–7, 9, 13, 26, 93–94, 113, 115, 120, 122–123, 141, 143, 145, 160, 171–172, 182–183, 202, 209, 222

Cerridwen, 56

chalice, 2, 72, 74, 84, 91, 93–94, 110, 130, 148–149

chaos theory, 38, 126

charcoal blocks, 76, 140–141, 148

Chayoth ha–Qadesh, 69–72, 120

Chesed, 125, 127, 129, 209, 211, 213

Chokmah, 125, 127, 129, 209, 211–214

clans, 203

cleanse, 38, 91, 141, 166, 187

cloak, 76, 103–104, 156, 181–184, 221

clockwise, 13, 88, 182

color, 14, 69–72, 116–121, 140, 175

consecrate, 73, 75, 108, 141, 165, 167, 191

consecrated water, 72, 92–93, 95, 97, 108, 110, 142, 144, 163, 166

Constantine, 203

contemplation, 6, 10, 13, 38, 54, 85–86, 99, 123, 171, 178, 197, 216

Council of Nicea, 57

counterclockwise, 88

coven, 42, 78, 93, 98, 159, 161, 197, 200

cowans, 49, 163

Craft, 20, 26, 35–36, 42, 82–83, 87, 92, 187, 198

creation, 11–13, 15, 55, 95, 111, 128–129, 131, 133–134, 149, 156, 180, 191, 219, 226

crone, 56

crystalglade, 200

Cu Chulainn, 60

cup, 66, 72, 74, 84, 91, 97, 100, 104, 110–111, 149

Da'ath, 124–125, 209, 212–214, 228

dagger, 73–74, 91, 93, 95, 97, 108, 163, 167

Dana, 56

dawn, 38, 66, 70, 90, 102–103, 137, 225

Demeter, 56

deosil, 88, 91, 94–95, 97, 100, 108–109, 182

Dion Fortune, 60, 206

Dionysis, 60, 123, 150

divination, 215–217, 232

Djinn, 71

dolly, 138

draw down the Moon, 56

dream, 80, 102, 104, 106, 169, 173, 177

dream diaries, 80

dreamer, 168–169, 229

dreams, 80, 160, 168–170

dreamscape, 200

Druids, 122, 203

eagle, 34, 46, 60, 72, 120

East, 70, 88–89, 91, 94

Eight Sabbats of the Wheel, 58

Eight-fold Wheel of the Year, 63

elder, 196

element, 81–84, 88, 92, 96–97, 110, 142, 147–149

elemental, 69–72, 88–90, 100, 140–141, 145–146, 148, 151, 165, 197, 216

elements, 20–22, 25, 27, 46, 68, 88, 92, 113, 120, 125, 147

emotional cripple, 188

enchantment, 59, 96, 182–184, 194

entity, 29, 33, 54, 146, 151, 164–166, 172–173

Ephemeredes, 175

Equinox, 58, 61–63

evocation, 207

evoke, 147, 194

evolving whole, 38, 82, 199

Excalibur, 70, 83

familiar, 88, 146, 172–173, 195

Feast of Bride, 58–59, 63

Feast of the Dead, 59

fetch, 146–148, 150–151

First Degree, 197

fith-fath, 138–141, 143–146, 167, 181

fith-fathing, 138–140, 189, 192

focus, 9, 34–35, 38–40, 83, 85, 87, 97, 139, 147, 149, 164, 166, 190, 210

Fool, 26, 216–217, 219, 222–226

Fool's Journey, 216, 219, 222–224, 226

four compass points, 88

four directions, 163

Gabriel, 72

Gaia, 56

Galahad, 60

gate, 28, 64, 89, 92, 94–95, 108–111, 116–117, 121, 141–143, 145, 149, 182–183, 195, 199, 226

Gates of the Elements, 88

gateway, 3, 88, 109, 151, 212, 214

geas, 175–176, 178, 200, 206

Geburah, 46, 125, 127, 129, 209–212

Gemini, 70, 227

getting, 29, 133, 164, 189–190, 192–193

getting rid of a thing, 164

Ghobb, 69

ghosts, 2, 157, 188, 201

gifts, 49, 146, 186–188

glamouring, 155–158, 200, 207

glamours, 156

Glyph of the Tree, 124

Gnomes, 69

goblet, 74, 91

Grail, 72, 84, 200, 222

Greater Sabbats, 58

Green Line, 197, 199

Green Man, 60, 204

grimoir, 121, 155

grimoire, 121, 155

ground, 9, 22, 34, 76, 93, 98, 101–102, 111, 142, 149, 157, 162, 164, 166, 182

guardian, 92, 109–111, 116–119, 158

Gwidion, 60

hauntings, 188

hazel, 75

healing, 138–139, 148, 154, 197, 229

Hecate, 56, 150

Hermetic Axiom, 69–72

Hermetic Quaternary, 81

Herne, 60, 150

High Priesthood, 99, 196–197

Hod, 125, 127, 129, 209–211

Holy Regalia, 69–72

I Ching, 175

Imbolc, 58

Inanna, 56

incantations, 84

incense, 70, 75–76, 85, 90–91, 93–94, 100, 108–109, 140–141, 144, 148–149, 154, 163, 181–182

initiation, 35, 49, 58–59, 62, 73, 98–101, 109–111, 196, 213, 222

intent, 11–12, 37–39, 50, 73, 82, 85, 87–88, 90–91, 100, 114, 139, 143, 145, 150, 163–164, 166–167, 184, 187, 190–191, 196

invisibility, 156, 181, 184, 207

invocation, 56, 158, 207

invoke, 73, 89, 100, 158, 199

invoking, 88, 91–92, 94–95, 100, 142–144, 149, 183

Ireland, 202–203

Ishtar, 56, 150

Isis, 56

Journey Between the Worlds, 102

Jupiter, 118, 123, 125, 211

Kabbala, 122

Kabbalah, 122

Kadaicha, 160–161

karma, 41

Kassandra, 176

keeping a thing out, 165

Kether, 124–127, 129, 209, 212–214, 228

king, 59–60, 62, 69–72

King of the Land, 60

King Stag, 60

Koori, 152, 160

la Rose Croix, 216

Ladder of Lights, 122

Lady, 55, 66, 140, 143, 145, 150–151, 158

landscape, 35, 53, 116, 169, 194

Law of Congruity, 16, 41–42, 124, 128, 207

Leo, 71, 227

Lesser Sabbats, 58, 61

Libra, 70, 227

lightning flash, 126–127, 212–213

Litha, 61

living the wheel, 61

Llugh, 60

Llughnassad, 58–59, 63

Lord, 60, 62, 140, 143, 145, 150–151, 158

Lord of Death, 60

Lord of Life, 60, 143

Lord of the Dance, 60

Lord of the Forests, 60

Lord of the Hunt, 60, 150

Lord of the Underworld, 60

Lucifer, 60

magic, 6, 9, 31, 35–37, 39, 41, 47–49, 53, 57–59, 64–65, 75, 81–82, 86, 97, 122, 128, 132, 138, 143, 152–153, 160, 169, 181, 187, 191–192, 194, 198–199, 204–205, 210, 215

magick, 123

magnet, 93

maiden, 56–57

Major Arcana, 215–216, 219, 227

Malkuth, 124–126, 129–130, 210–211, 214, 228

Mari, 56, 60, 212

Mars, 118, 125, 211

matrix, 7–8, 55, 123, 210

meditation, 6–7, 10, 12–13, 15, 114, 172–173

Mercury, 116, 125, 210–211

Merlin, 60, 64–65

Michael, 71

midday, 71, 90, 117

midnight, 69, 90, 96, 103

mindscape, 6–8, 10, 168

Moon, 49, 52, 54, 56–58, 62–66, 74–75, 88, 94, 105, 116, 121, 125, 136, 147, 164, 182, 194, 197–198, 201, 207, 209, 225, 228

moon phase, 147

Morgan le-fey, 56

Morrigan, 152

Mother, 29, 56, 61, 123, 140, 160, 188, 204–205, 217

Möbius, 133

Mulengro, 28–30, 155–156, 187, 206–207

name, 2, 28–29, 35, 98–99, 101, 105–112, 137, 179–180, 229–231

necklace, 99–100, 109–110

Nehushtan, 126

Nemesis, 56

Nemet, 5, 37

Nephesh, 124–125, 127–128

Neschamah, 124–125, 127–128, 133

Netzach, 125, 127, 129, 209–211

New Moon, 57, 74, 194

Nixsa, 72

numerology, 81, 228–229, 232

O. B. E., 171

occult, 11–12, 27, 36, 75, 82, 114, 122, 155–156, 160, 175–176, 198, 210

ochre, 147

Odin, 60, 123

oil, 76–77, 92–94, 97, 100, 110–111, 147, 182, 191

oracle, 52, 232

Oracular, 175, 216

orifices, 164, 166

Osiris, 60, 123

Ostara, 61

Otz Chim, 122

Ouija, 160, 162

out-of-body, 169, 171

Pan, 60, 123, 150

pathworking, 216

Pegasus, 152

pentacle, 69, 74–75, 82, 91, 93–94, 96, 108–110, 130, 140, 144, 148, 197

pentagram, 74, 88, 91–92, 94–95, 97, 99–100, 108–110, 119, 142–145, 149, 151, 164, 166, 182–184, 189

Persephone, 56

personal power, 6, 35, 39, 206

Pisces, 72, 228

plaiting, 148, 190

planetary symbolism, 209, 215

planets, 60, 120, 126, 128, 194–195

poppet, 138, 144–145

portent, 177

preparation, 37, 39, 73, 76, 87, 99–100, 140

priest, 52, 62, 108–110, 112, 158, 199, 201

priestess, 52, 56, 59, 62, 64–65, 108–110, 112, 158, 199–200, 206, 213, 219 priesthood, 26, 41, 47, 49, 51, 53, 61, 99, 196–199

protection, 142, 156, 163, 166–167, 185–186, 188–189

psi–empathic, 185

psi–empathy, 158, 185, 187

psychic attack, 188–189

psychic protection, 156, 185–186, 189

Qabbalah, 29, 81, 122, 190

Qbblh, 122

QBL, 122

Qliphoth, 29

quantum physics, 126, 215

quest, 6, 35, 37, 40, 53, 81, 104, 118–119, 156, 198, 222

Raphael, 70

realm of dreams, 168

realms of accessibility, 113, 197

Red Line, 198–199

reiving, 85–87, 163–164, 184, 187

Robin Hood, 60

Ruach, 124–125, 127, 209

runes, 175

runestones, 175

Sabbat, 58, 63, 78

Sabbats, 58, 61–63

Sacred Marriage, 59

sacred space, 37, 75, 88, 90, 100

Sagittarius, 71, 227

salamanders, 71

salt, 69, 77, 87, 90–92, 105, 108, 140–142, 166

Samhain, 58–59, 62–64

Saturn, 119, 125, 195, 211–212, 231–232

Scorpio, 72, 227

seal, 74, 88–89, 91, 93–95, 120, 143, 146, 150, 164–167

sealing wax, 165

Second Degree, 198

Sephirah, 124, 129–130

Sephiroth, 114, 124, 126–129, 228

service, 40, 229

Shaitan, 60

shaman, 153

Shamash, 60

shapeshifting, 102, 152–155, 172

Sheila na gig, 204

sigils, 74–75, 119, 159, 167

silence, 6, 8–10, 34, 38, 72, 84, 94, 108, 114, 206, 219

skyclad, 76, 141, 148

solar cycle, 147

solitary, 25, 84, 98, 141

solstice, 58, 61–63, 194–195

Sophia, 56

sorcerers, 203

sorcery, 26, 47, 56, 113, 135, 139, 152, 157, 194

spear, 71, 83

Spell, 8, 79, 138–139, 143, 146, 148, 150–151, 181–182, 184, 191–192

spellcrafting, 8, 11, 42, 83–84, 90, 134–135, 168, 189, 194, 216

spells, 7, 79, 84, 148, 155, 190, 192

spheres, 121, 124

spring, 59, 61–63, 65, 70

Spring Equinox, 61, 63

staff, 71, 74, 77, 130, 198

star, 49, 60, 126, 197, 199, 212, 224, 227

summer, 59, 61–63, 71, 194–195

summon, 15, 65, 73, 88, 90, 92, 94–95, 141–143, 145, 149, 151, 153, 166, 189, 192, 194

Sun, 49, 52, 58–59, 62, 88, 94–95, 104, 116–117, 125, 127, 138, 188, 197–198, 209, 212, 224–225

sunset, 72, 90, 99–100

sunwise, 88

sword, 50, 66, 70, 83, 96, 130, 197, 199, 201, 203, 221

swords, 70, 227

sylphs, 70

Synod of Whitby, 203

talismans, 99, 165, 167

Tarot, 7, 69–72, 81, 124, 170, 175–176, 179–180, 213, 215–217, 226

tattooing, 203

Taurus, 69, 227

temple, 34, 84–85, 90–91, 194

therianthropic, 152

Therianthropism, 152, 154

Third Degree, 199

Thor, 60

thurible, 75

Tiamat, 56

timescape, 7, 169, 209

Tiphareth, 125, 127, 129, 209–214

to dare, 71, 81, 83

to know, 3, 19, 29, 39–41, 48–49, 65, 68–69, 81–82, 84, 111, 120, 128, 137–138, 152–153, 157, 190, 199, 204, 206, 212

tools, 6, 29, 69–73, 77, 100, 147, 161, 168, 178, 232

training, 11–12, 18, 42, 62, 83, 153, 175, 185, 196–198, 200, 206

Tree, 75, 114, 122–133, 154, 170, 209–215, 228

Tree of Life, 114, 122, 125, 129, 209–215, 228

Underworld, 54, 56, 59–60, 62, 119

Uranus, 120, 125, 212–214

Uriel, 69

vampire, 187

vampires, 186

vampirism, 186–187

veil, 2, 120, 133, 156, 219

Venus, 60, 75, 117, 125, 210

vessel, 8, 36, 39, 53, 74, 76, 91, 127, 143, 158, 196

vial, 77, 93–94, 100, 110

Virgo, 69, 227

visualization, 11–15, 83, 91, 99, 114, 154, 172

visualize, 11–15, 114, 149, 151, 172, 184

Vivienne, 56

wand, 71, 74–75, 83, 91, 93–94, 142–143, 145, 148–149, 151

wands, 71, 75, 227

waning, 56, 58, 194

ward, 165–166

warding, 165–166, 189

warlock, 47

waxing, 56, 62, 194

web, 39, 87

white cord, 90, 100, 140, 181

will, 4–6, 8–10, 13, 15–18, 20, 25–29, 31–32, 35, 37–42, 48–50, 52, 56, 58, 68, 70, 73–88, 90–101, 103–104, 107–108, 111, 113–121, 127–128, 131–133, 136, 138–148, 150–159, 163–168, 170–179, 181–200, 202, 204, 206, 209, 213–217, 219, 226, 232

wine, 2, 74, 86, 93, 97,
    99–100, 110, 148–149,
    151, 191

winged bull, 69, 120

winter, 59, 61–63, 69, 75,
    102, 194–195

Winter Solstice, 61–63,
    194–195

with the sun, 88

world, 7, 30, 41, 49, 56,
    64–66, 99, 102, 121–123,
    130, 136–137, 194, 196,
    198–199, 202, 226

worlds, 39, 122, 124,
    129–130, 132, 169, 190,
    194

Yeheshuah, 60, 123

Yesod, 125, 127, 129,
    209–211

Yetzirah, 125, 129–133

Yggdrasil, 122

yule, 61

Zeus, 60, 123

zodiac, 69–72, 120, 126

Zohar, 122

## Free Magazine

Read unique articles by Llewellyn authors, recommendations by experts, and information on new releases. To receive a **free** copy of Llewellyn's consumer magazine, *New Worlds of Mind & Spirit,* simply call 1-877-NEW-WRLD or visit our website at www.llewellyn.com and click on *New Worlds.*

# ☾ LLEWELLYN ORDERING INFORMATION

### Order Online:
Visit our website at www.llewellyn.com, select your books, and order them on our secure server.

### Order by Phone:
- Call toll-free within the U.S. at 1-877-NEW-WRLD (1-877-639-9753). Call toll-free within Canada at 1-866-NEW-WRLD (1-866-639-9753)
- We accept VISA, MasterCard, and American Express

### Order by Mail:
Send the full price of your order (MN residents add 7% sales tax) in U.S. funds, plus postage & handling to:

> **Llewellyn Worldwide**
> **P.O. Box 64383, Dept. 1-56718-782-x**
> **St. Paul, MN 55164-0383, U.S.A.**

## Postage & Handling:

**Standard** (U.S., Mexico, & Canada). If your order is:
  $49.99 and under, add $3.00
  $50.00 and over, FREE STANDARD SHIPPING

AK, HI, PR: $15.00 for one book plus $1.00 for each additional book.

**International Orders** (airmail only):
  $16.00 for one book plus $3.00 for each additional book

*Orders are processed within 2 business days.*
*Please allow for normal shipping time. Postage and handling rates subject to change.*

## Buckland's Complete Book of Witchcraft

RAYMOND BUCKLAND

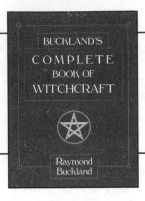

Here is the most complete resource to the study and practice of modern, nondenominational Wicca. This is a lavishly illustrated, self-study course for the solitary or group. Included are rituals; exercises for developing psychic talents; information on all major "sects" of the Craft; sections on tools, beliefs, dreams, meditations, divination, herbal lore, healing, ritual clothing, and much, much more. This book unites theory and practice into a comprehensive course designed to help you develop into a practicing Witch, one of the "Wise Ones." It is written by Ray Buckland, a very famous and respected authority on Witchcraft who first came public with the Old Religion in the United States. Large format with workbook-type exercises, profusely illustrated and full of music and chants. Takes you from A to Z in the study of Witchcraft.

Never before has so much information on the Craft of the Wise been collected in one place. Traditionally, there are three degrees of advancement in most Wiccan traditions. When you have completed studying this book, you will be the equivalent of a Third-Degree Witch. Even those who have practiced Wicca for years find useful information in this book, and many covens are using this for their textbook. If you want to become a Witch, or if you merely want to find out what Witchcraft is really about, you will find no better book than this.

0-87542-050-8, 368 pp.
8½ x 11, illus.                                                                 $17.95

## Italian Witchcraft

### The Old Religion of Southern Europe

### RAVEN GRIMASSI

Discover the rich legacy of magick and ritual handed down by Italian witches through the generations. Trace the roots of the Italian Pagan tradition as it survives the times, confronted by Christianity, revived in the fourteenth century by the Holy Strega, and passed on as the Legend of Aradia to the present day. Explore the secrets of Janarra (lunar) witches, Tanarra (star) witches, and Fanarra (ley lines) witches. Their ancient wisdoms come together in the modern Aridian tradition, presented here for both theoretical understanding and everyday practice. You will learn the gospel of Aradia, and the powerful practice of "casting shadows," an ancient tradition only now available to the public. *Italian Witchcraft* also gives you the practical how-tos of modern Strega traditions, including making tools, casting and breaking spells, seasonal and community rites, honoring the Watchers, creating a Spirit Flame, and much more.

1-56718-259-3, 336 pp.
7½ x 9⅛, illus.                                                         $14.95

To order, call 1-877-NEW-WRLD

Prices subject to change without notice

**Living Wicca**

A Further Guide for the Solitary Practitioner

SCOTT CUNNINGHAM

*Living Wicca* is the long–awaited sequel to Scott Cunningham's wildly successful *Wicca: a Guide for the Solitary Practitioner.* This book is for those who have made the conscious decision to bring their Wiccan spirituality into their everyday lives. It provides solitary practitioners with the tools and added insights that will enable them to blaze their own spiritual paths—to become their own high priests and priestesses.

*Living Wicca* takes a philosophical look at the questions, practices, and differences within Witchcraft. It covers the various tools of learning available to the practitioner, the importance of secrecy in one's practice, guidelines to performing ritual when ill, magical names, initiation, and the Mysteries. It discusses the benefits of daily prayer and meditation, making offerings to the gods, how to develop a prayerful attitude, and how to perform Wiccan rites when away from home or in emergency situations.

Unlike any other book on the subject, *Living Wicca* is a step-by-step guide to creating your own Wiccan tradition and personal vision of the gods, designing your personal ritual and symbols, developing your own book of shadows, and truly living your Craft.

0-87542-184-9, 208 pp.
6 x 9, illus. $12.95

## Covencraft

Witchcraft for Three or More

### Amber K

Here is the complete guidebook for anyone who desires to practice Witchcraft in a caring, challenging, well-organized spiritual support group: a coven. Whether you hope to learn more about this ancient spiritual path, are a coven member wanting more rewarding experiences in your group, are looking for a coven to join, are thinking of starting one, or are a Wiccan elder gathering proven techniques and fresh ideas—this book is for you.

Amber K shares what she as learned about beginning and maintaining healthy covens in her twenty years as a Wiccan priestess. Learn what a coven is, how it works, and how you can make your coven experience more effective, enjoyable, and rewarding. Plus, get practical hands-on guidance in the form of sample Articles of Incorporation, Internet resources, sample by-laws, and sample budgets. Seventeen ritual scripts are also provided.

1-56718-018-3, 480 pp.
7 x 10, illus.                                                                                      $19.95

The Witch's Coven

Finding & Forming Your Own Circle

EDAIN McCOY

*The Witch's Coven* gives you an insider's look at how a real Witch's coven operates, from initiation and secret vows to parting rituals. You'll get step-by-step guidance for joining or forming a coven, plus sage advice and exclusive insights to help you decide which group is the right one for you.

Maybe you're thinking about joining a coven, but don't know what to expect, or how to make contacts. Perhaps you already belong to a coven, but your group needs ideas for organizing a teaching circle or mediating conflicts. Either way, you're sure to find *The Witch's Coven* a practical source of wisdom.

Joining a coven can be an important step in your spiritual life. Before you take that step, let a practicing Witch lead you through the hidden inner workings of a Witch's coven.

**0-7387-0388-5, 224 pp.**
**5¼ x 8**                                                          **$12.95**

To order, call 1-877-NEW-WRLD
Prices subject to change without notice